BEATING A DEAD HORSE

Jenny Stafford

BROADWAY PLAY PUBLISHING INC
New York
www.broadwayplaypublishing.com
info@broadwayplaypublishing.com

BEATING A DEAD HORSE
© Copyright 2023 Jenny Stafford

Cover art by DALL-E

First edition: March 2023
I S B N: 978-0-88145-971-5

Book design: Marie Donovan
Page make-up: Adobe InDesign
Typeface: Palatino

For Marmadillo, Dadoo, and Pookie

BEATING A DEAD HORSE had a workshop production Athena Project (Artistic Director, Angela Astle) 2-8 April 2017. The cast and creative contributor were:

STEVE .... Tony Ryan
MARTY .... Ben Hilzer
BRYONY .... Leslie Randle
ERICA .... Alexis Robbins
TODD .... Sean Michael Cummings
MARIANNE .... Carol Bloom
MARCUS/FRITZ .... Anthony Adu

Director .... Penny Cole

BEATING A DEAD HORSE was originally presented by the Bloomington Playwrights Project (Artistic Director, Chad Rabinovitz; Associate Artistic Director, Ben Smith) from 29 September-14 October 2017. The cast and creative contributors were:

STEVE ....Michael Sheehan
MARTY ....Marcus Kearns
BRYONY...Carina Lastimosa
ERICa...Ali Lidbury
TODD...Henry McDaniel
MARIANNE ....Kate Braun
FRITZ/MARCUS...Steve Scott

Director ....Ivey Lowe
Sound design...Joel Watson
Set design ....David Wade
Lighting design ....Erica Johnson
Costume design...Chib Gratz
Fabricator ....Nicole Bruce
Prop Master ....Barb Steininger

CHARACTERS & SETTING

STEVE, *30s. Meek, mild, kind owner of a failing pet funeral home. Always tries to do the right thing.*

MARTY, *30s.* STEVE'*s brother. Charming, corrupt, smooth-talker. Recently got out of jail.*

BRYONY, *30s.* STEVE'*s girlfriend. Funny, sassy, doesn't take crap from anyone—but with a soft side.*

ERICA, *30s. Attractive, down-on-her-luck actress, a hard edge to her.*

TODD, *30s. Optimistic, hopeful, and eager, but not too bright. Trying to start a taxidermy business, but he's terrible at taxidermy.*

MARIANNE, *60s. An old, eccentric, rich racehorse owner.*

FRITZ/MARCUS, *any age.* FRITZ *is* MARIANNE'*s butler. Proper and reserved.* MARCUS *is a surfer dude who* FRITZ *impersonates.*

The fictional town of Beavercreek, Pennsylvania. A small, sad pet funeral home adjoined to a small, sad house.

NOTE ON MUSIC

For performance of copyrighted songs, arrangements
or recordings referenced in this play, permission
of the copyright owner(s) must be obtained. Other
songs, arrangements or recordings may be substituted
provided permission from the copyright owner(s) of
such songs, arrangements or recordings is obtained,
or songs, arrangements or recordings in the public
domain may be substituted.

ACT ONE

Scene One

(A blank stage. STEVE *and* MARTY *sit center stage in side-by-side chairs, staring straight ahead.* STEVE *sits slightly slumped over, his messy hair getting in his eyes as he tries to push up his glasses. He seems nervous. Next to him,* MARTY *sits tall and strong, the picture of confidence. He has a charming smile.)*

STEVE: *(Stiffly)* Hi. I'm Steve Martin. No, not that Steve Martin. A different…Steve…Martin.

MARTY: And I'm Martin Martin. *(Beat)* Our parents were jerks.

*(*MARTY *smiles, and* STEVE *leaps forward to turn off a video camera.)*

STEVE: Marty! I told you, we have to do this in one take! Be serious!

MARTY: We want people to like us, right?

STEVE: We want people to *trust* us. Now do it right. *(He turns on the camera again and sits stiffly back in his chair.)* Hi. I'm Steve Martin. No, not that Steve Martin. A diff—

MARTY: And I'm Martin Martin.

STEVE & MARTY: And we're the owners of "A Nice Farm Upstate With Plenty of Room To Run Around" Pet Funeral Home.

MARTY: *(Under his breath)* It's too long. It's always been too long.

STEVE: *(Ignoring him)* We know losing your pet can be a traumatic experience, and we're here to ease you and your pet through this difficult time.

MARTY: Our father founded this business in 1970—

STEVE: *(Coughing to correct him)* 1972—

MARTY: —1972, so you know a proud family business is the only place to take your family business.

STEVE & MARTY: Our services include—

(STEVE pauses the camera.)

STEVE: I told you, I'm doing the list of services! You only have two lines!

MARTY: What?! This whole thing was my idea! You never have any ideas! Why did you get to write the script?! *(He pulls it out and flips through it.)* How many times can you say "business?" Sounds like you're talking about taking a dump!

STEVE: Fine. *Fine.* You read the list of services. But if you mispronounce "cremation" again, you're done. *(He turns the camera on again.)* Hi. I'm Steve Martin.

MARTY: Aw, come on! I'm not doing all that again!

STEVE: I don't know how to edit it!

MARTY: You'll figure it out. Let's just go. *(He looks at the camera and gives a charming smile.)* Our services include cremation, pet caskets, fully catered funeral services, burial in our pet cemetery, calming ceremonies to transition your pet from life to death, and a wide range of memorabilia to commemorate your pet's face, or, if you prefer, nose, paw, or talon print.

(STEVE stops the camera.)

STEVE: Why are you doing your sexy voice? Who says "talon" like that?!

MARTY: Who says "talon" at all?! What is my life?!

STEVE: Just stop being sexy. Nothing about this should be sexy.

MARTY: Then you should do it yourself.

STEVE: Can we just wrap this up? (*He leans forward and starts the camera again.*) So come see us for all of your pet aftercare needs.

MARTY: So that when you tell your kids that their pet went to "A Nice Farm Upstate With Plenty of Room to Run Around," you won't be lying.

STEVE: (*Singing an awkward jingle*) "A Nice Farm Upstate With Plenty of Room to Run Around."

(MARTY *and* STEVE *give the camera a winning smile. Blackout.*)

Scene Two

(*Lights up on a split stage. We see that the Pet Funeral Home [stage right] is attached to the house [Stage left] by a door in between them, center. The Pet Funeral Home is a bleak, bleak place. A counter stands center. The walls are lined with "animal obituaries," complete with pictures. A shelf to the side holds a variety of tiny caskets. There are two cushy seats in a comforting "sitting area," with a window to the outside. A door upstage says "Employees Only." A door connects it to the living room/kitchen of the home, stage left—an equally bleak place. A living room and a kitchen are visible, in dowdy, retro colors.* BRYONY *sits in the kitchen, carving an eggplant with an exactoknife. She wears an apron and a kerchief in her hair, and is extremely focused.*)

TODD: Knock, knock!

BRYONY: *(Not looking up)* Hey, Todd! Come on in!

TODD: Hey, Bryony! Steve or Marty here?

BRYONY: No, they're over at the pet funeral home.

TODD: Shoot. I wanted to show them my latest creation.

BRYONY: Oh, no, please don't bring any of that stuff in here! You know how it creeps me out!

TODD: No, no, no! This one's good! *(He exits and re-enters with a grotesquely taxidermied deer head. The eyes are far too wide and point in different directions, the antlers are all askew, and its mouth is twisted in a perpetually perplexed look.)* See?

(BRYONY gasps in horror.)

BRYONY: Oh my God!

TODD: It's good, right? Way better than the last one.

BRYONY: Well, this one has both eyes, so…that's something.

TODD: It's not perfect, I know, but I'm working on it. Todd's Taxidermy is on the rise! What are you working on? Something for the diner?

BRYONY: No, this is for my business. There's this petting zoo opening in Artinville, and I'm doing the food for the party, so I'm making a penguin out of an eggplant. I have to make forty of them by Saturday.

TODD: Aw, look at us! Both making animals! *(He holds up his deer head. Beat)*

BRYONY: Yeah.

(Focus shifts to stage right to the pet funeral home, where STEVE stands behind the counter, and MARCUS, a chill "surfer dude," stands other side of the counter with a shoebox.)

MARCUS: I dunno, man. He was like, fine, and then he was like, dead.

STEVE: I'm so sorry to hear that.

MARCUS: And I was like, "Lil' dude, don't go!" And he was like, "I'm a cat! I used all my lives and my time on earth is finite!" And I was like, "Duuuude!" And he was like, "Peace." And then he was gone.

(STEVE *lifts the lid of the shoebox and recoils.*)

STEVE: I really am very sorry for your loss.

MARCUS: No biggie. *(He gets emotional.)* Losin' your best friend in the world…no biggie.

STEVE: Losing a pet is always hard. We can give him a proper send-off, though. You have several options. We could cremate him and put him in an urn, so you can sprinkle his ashes somewhere he liked to go—

MARCUS: He always wanted to see the ocean.

(Beat)

STEVE: So, that's an option. Or we have a lovely selection of caskets in his size. They range from this pine casket, at twenty-five dollars, up to this chrome casket at a hundred and twenty-five dollars. What were you looking for?

MARCUS: Um…what can I get for like, five dollars? *(He starts digging though his pockets.)*

STEVE: Well…um…

MARCUS: Oh, dude! I totally left my wallet at the smoothie place!

STEVE: We have a smoothie place?

MARCUS: No, man. I make my own smoothies at my house.

STEVE: So your wallet is…

MARCUS: At my house. In my kitchen. The smoothie place. I'll be back.

(MARCUS *leaves the shoebox on the counter and runs out.* STEVE *looks at the shoebox apprehensively. He tentatively lifts the lid again, shudders, and drops it.* BRYONY *pokes her head through the door between the house and the pet funeral home.*)

BRYONY: Psst! Steve! Todd brought his taxidermy over again! Come save me!

STEVE: I wish I could—I'm with a customer!

BRYONY: Really?! Oh baby, I'm so proud of you! *(She runs over and gives him a quick kiss.)* Wow, it really reeks in here. It smells like…money for the engagement ring fund!

STEVE: *(Falsely enthusiastic)* Yay!

BRYONY: Yay! *(She kisses him again.)* I'll let you get to it! Please come save me from Todd when you're done… he says this one's a deer, but I'm not convinced.

(BRYONY *exits back through the door to the house where* TODD *sits proudly with his deer head. She returns to her work in the kitchen, and* MARTY *enters the house from the outside, his head tipped back drinking a beer. When he brings his head back down, he is face to face with the deer head.*)

MARTY: Oh, jeez!

TODD: It's good, right?!

MARTY: It is…not as bad as…I mean, it has… *(Beat)* No, I can't. It's what nightmares are made of, Todd. Where are its ears?

TODD: I accidentally cut one off, then figured, well, it can't have *one* ear, right? That would look nuts. But I got a *lot* less blood in my house making this one, so I do think I'm getting better. I'm gonna keep practicing, business partner.

MARTY: We're not business partners.

TODD: But we *will* be. When I get good, people will pay to have their pets preserved for all time. I looked it up. It's a thing.

(Focus shifts back to the Pet Funeral Home. Its front door opens, and ERICA enters. She is pretty, with big curly hair and a big smile. She wears cutoff shorts and cowboy boots, and pulls a suitcase behind her.)

ERICA: Hello?

STEVE: Hi, can I help you?

ERICA: I'm just looking for—Steve! Steve Martin!

STEVE: Yes, but not the one you think.

ERICA: It's Erica. Erica Meyers? We…went to high school together?

STEVE: Oh, yeah! Long time no see!

(STEVE comes around the counter and gives ERICA a hug.)

ERICA: Yeah, I just got back to town. I'm looking for my brother, Todd—I stopped by the house but he wasn't there, and I know you guys are friends—is he here?

STEVE: Oh, he's—

(MARTY enters from the house, drinking his beer. He interrupts them.)

MARTY: Hey, I just thought of the best promotion! It's called "The Dog Days of Summer." If your dog dies in July or August, you get twenty percent off!

STEVE: Close the door. Look who it is!

(MARTY stops in his tracks. He smiles.)

MARTY: Erica Meyers.

ERICA: Martin Squared!

(ERICA runs across the room and gives MARTY a huge hug.)

MARTY: Are you what smells in here?!

ERICA: God, I hope not! Though I was on a bus all night!

STEVE: It's not her. It's business. *(He points to the box.)*

MARTY: We got a customer?! Thank *God*! Let's make some money in this place! Oooh, boy! *(He starts to do a dance.)*

ERICA: I bet your dad's proud to see you take over the family business.

MARTY: He's not. Both because he's not proud, and because he's dead.

STEVE: Marty...

ERICA: Oh. Jeez. I'm so sorry. I'm...sure he was proud though.

MARTY: Of Steve maybe. I was a pain in that man's ass for years.

(ERICA snickers.)

ERICA: Like that time in high school when you got suspended for running a cheating ring out of the boy's bathroom?

STEVE: Ha, I—

ERICA: Or that time we stole my dad's goat and hung it from the ceiling at prom like a disco ball?

MARTY: That was the night I learned you could bedazzle a goat.

STEVE: And—

ERICA: And that twine will only hold a goat up for about twenty minutes.

(ERICA and MARTY laugh. STEVE sighs, annoyed at being left out of the conversation. He picks up the box.)

STEVE: Speaking of animals that have been mistreated, I'm just gonna take this in the back and put it on ice.

MARTY: *(Waving him away)* Yeah, okay.

(STEVE exits through the back "Employees Only" door.)

MARTY: I thought you were some big city actress in Philadelphia or something!

ERICA: More like a professional couch surfer. Casting couch.

MARTY: Oh. Wow.

ERICA: I'm kidding. My biggest gig in ten years was a radio ad for carpet cleaner. Figured it wasn't happening.

MARTY: Darlin', you do not belong on the radio.

ERICA: *(Blushing)* Thanks.

(MARCUS re-enters the Pet Funeral Home from the outside door.)

MARCUS: Ok, got my wallet back from the smoothie place. At first I thought somebody stole it from the smoothie place, then I was like wait, I live alone. *(He proudly places it on the counter and looks around.)* Where's Steve Carrell and my cat?

(STEVE re-enters from the "Employees Only" door.)

STEVE: We're right here. I was just taking some measurements.

MARTY: Will you excuse us for a minute?

(MARTY quickly pulls STEVE off into the house so fast that STEVE almost drops the cat box. ERICA and MARCUS are left alone in the funeral home. They sit together awkwardly. Focus shifts to the house.)

MARTY: You said we had business! It's a hippie with cat!

STEVE: So? It's a customer!

MARTY: This is why we're broke! Why can't we ever get an elephant or something in here?!

STEVE: Yeah, with all the dead elephants in Pennsylvania.

(Focus shifts to the funeral home. MARCUS *turns to* ERICA.)

MARCUS: Hi. I'm Marcus.

ERICA: Hey. Erica.

(MARCUS *looks* ERICA *up and down.)*

MARCUS: Hey, Erica.

(ERICA *smiles uncomfortably.)*

ERICA: I'm just gonna…I have to…um…I'll be back.

MARCUS: Really?

(Beat)

ERICA: No. *(She backs away and heads into the house.)* Sorry, that guy was creeping me out! *(She looks around and sees the group.)* Hey, everyone!

TODD: Hey, sis! You're back!

ERICA: Hi, Bryony!

BRYONY: *(Focused on* STEVE*)* Hey, Erica. *(She crosses to* STEVE.)* Steve, are you botching the sale again?! Do you want to live in this house forever? Do you want us to live with Marty forever? No offense, Marty.

MARTY: None taken. I'm trying to get away from you guys too. *(He picks up an eggplant from off the counter and takes a bite of it, like an apple.)*

BRYONY: Don't eat that eggplant! It has to be a penguin!

MARTY: You have like, forty of them.

BRYONY: THEY ALL HAVE TO BE PENGUINS! This is what I'm talking about! I can't live in this house and run my catering business out of this house! I want to get married and start our life!

ERICA: You guys aren't married yet?

STEVE: We don't want to rush into anything.

(All overlapping:)

TODD: You've been dating since the fourth grade/

MARTY: She's literally been your girlfriend for twenty-two years/

BRYONY: I'M THIRTY-TWO!

STEVE: Can we all just calm down? The guy hasn't even decided what he's getting yet.

MARTY: Oh really? *(He gives a smile and cracks his knuckles.)* Then watch and learn, my friend.

(MARTY grabs STEVE and pulls him back towards the Pet Funeral Home, then turns back.)

MARTY: Oh, yeah—Erica's back! Wait here.

(MARTY and STEVE enter the Pet Funeral Home, and MARTY solemnly approaches MARCUS.)

MARTY: Thank you for your patience. I'm so sorry to hear about the loss of…

MARCUS: Orange Marcus.

MARTY: I'm sorry?

MARCUS: I'm Marcus. He was Orange Marcus.

(Beat. Focus splits so we are watching both scenes at once.)

TODD: Welcome back, sis! Hold this. *(He hands her the deer head and crosses to BRYONY.)* Hey Bryony, I bet all this new business is because of their commercial. I saw it at three-thirty last night on the public access channel. There's a lot of pickling acid fumes in my house; it's really messed up my sleep cycle. But it looked real good. You'd never even know Marty just got out of jail!

ERICA: Marty was in jail?

(MARTY *smoothly put his arm around* MARCUS'S
shoulders.)

MARTY: What better way send him off to the next life in
comfort than with a beautiful casket?

MARCUS: I'm pretty strapped for cash, dude.

MARTY: Hmmm. Well, was Orange Marcus a plain old
cat, or a special cat?

MARCUS: Dude, did you not look in the box? He was...
like...you know...like...

(MARCUS *can't find a word good enough to describe his cat.*
MARTY *loses patience and cuts him off.*)

MARTY: Well that changes everything. I was going to
say we could give him one of these pine boxes. But if
he was a special cat...why not get a pendant with his
name on it? (*He smoothly grabs a display pendant and
displays it proudly.*)

BRYONY: He tried to catch rain and sell it as Beaver
Creek Bottled Beaver Water.

MARTY: We could engrave his name right here. Or a
t-shirt with his picture. Or a mug. Or a sandstone urn.

ERICA: How long was he in jail?

TODD: Thirty days.

MARTY: Just something so he knows he'll be
remembered.

BRYONY: Then he kind of punched a cop while he was
in there, so they added two years and eleven months.

ERICA: Wow. Three years.

(MARTY *dramatically steps forward, really putting on a
show.*)

MARTY: Because really, isn't that all any of us want? To
know that when we're gone, we won't be forgotten?

That we mattered? That tiny, insignificant lives counted for something?

MARCUS: *(Crying out, swept up in the drama)* I'll take it! I'll take all of it! I love you, Orange Marcus!

(MARTY swiftly moves back behind the counter and rattles off prices with the speed of a used car salesman.)

MARTY: Great. The casket is a hundred and twenty-five dollars, the pendant is fifty dollars, the T-shirt and the mug are thirty dollars each, bringing your total to two hundred and thirty-five dollars.

MARCUS: Whooooah, dude. You think I can spend two hundred bucks on a cat?! I only make like, fifty bucks a week at the smoothie place.

MARTY: We have a smoothie place?

MARCUS: No, I make them in my house. But then sometimes I sell them to people. You guys should come by sometime!

STEVE: So…we do have a smoothie place.

MARTY: Well that's perfect! You bring us half of your earnings, and in only two months you'll have given Orange Marcus the goodbye he deserves.

MARCUS: Can I think about it?

MARTY: Well, it seems like it should be an easy decision—

(STEVE has had enough.)

STEVE: Ahem! Of course you can think about it.

MARTY: I'll go get started on your commemorative pendant. *(He turns to leave out of the "Employees Only" entrance, then turns back to STEVE, under his breath—)* Cha-CHING!

STEVE: Close the door!

(MARTY *reaches back out and closes the door to the*
"Employees Only" entrance. A moment)

STEVE: You don't...Orange Marcus was a special cat, no
matter what you decide to get.

MARCUS: I just don't want him to like, look up from cat
hell and think I didn't love him.

(MARCUS *sits sadly in one of the chairs, and* STEVE *sits in
the other one.*)

MARCUS: Especially 'cuz he was about to give birth
to Marcus the Third. Or Striped Marcus. Or Calico
Marcus. I was gonna wait and see; I don't know who
his dad was. Just like me.

STEVE: It's always hard when we lose someone we love.
But...I think whenever we see something that reminds
us of them, that's their way of looking down on us, and
staying with us.

(*Beat*)

MARCUS: I can bring half my pay every week.

(STEVE *sighs.*)

STEVE: You know...I think maybe Marty didn't know
how special he was. Because...we give free caskets to
really special cats.

MARCUS: (*Perking up*) Really?

STEVE: Really. (*He heads to the shelf and reaches for one of
the pine caskets.*)

MARCUS: The really nice chrome ones?

(STEVE *freezes.*)

STEVE: Of course!

(STEVE *takes a chrome casket off the shelf and hands it to*
MARCUS.)

MARCUS: Thanks, dude! *(He extends a hand to shake, then gets overcome and throws his arms around* STEVE, *giving him a big hug and hitting him in the stomach with the chrome box.)* You're the nicest guy in the whole world. Your next smoothie is on me.

*(*STEVE *doubles over in pain, returning the hug.)*

STEVE: *(Gasping)* No big thing.

*(*MARCUS *exits, and* STEVE *stands a moment in pain.)*

STEVE: No. Big. Thing.

(Focus shifts back to the house.)

TODD: Well, I'm gonna head home and go to bed.

BRYONY: It's six-thirty.

TODD: Pickling agent sleep cycle.

ERICA: Todd, I can stay with you, right?

TODD: Of course! I mean, quick heads up, I've turned the whole house into my…business center.

ERICA: Meaning…

TODD: There's a dead moose in your room. But I can skootch him right over!

ERICA: Great…

BRYONY: You can stay here, Erica. The couch pulls out.

ERICA: Really? Is that ok with you guys? I'm really quiet, I promise.

TODD: You guys are the best. *(He bends down to pick up the deer head.)* Ugh, this thing's like sixty pounds. Can I just leave it here?

ERICA & BRYONY: No!

TODD: Got it.

*(*TODD *picks up the head and exits. A moment)*

BRYONY: It's pretty quiet over there--I'm gonna go make sure Steve isn't screwing up the sale. Make yourself at home!

(BRYONY *crosses into the Pet Funeral Home, where* STEVE *is sitting in one of the chairs. A moment*)

BRYONY: Did you…make the big sale?

STEVE: Um…he decided to make other arrangements.

(BRYONY *looks around the room.*)

BRYONY: One of the caskets is missing. You gave it to him, didn't you?!

STEVE: I'm sorry! But this guy was…so sad, and he didn't have any money, and Marty was trying to swindle him, and…maybe he'll come back?

BRYONY: He's not coming back!

STEVE: He might come back.

BRYONY: You gave him everything he wanted for free! You lost the sale! He's not coming back! (*She sits in the chair next to* STEVE, *with her fingers to her temples.*) It's okay, Steve. You're a good man. And I'd rather have a good man than…enough money to quit the diner and start my own business with a cute little sign over the door with my name on it.

STEVE: You work so hard.

BRYONY: Well, maybe someday I can quit the diner and just do my own business. (*Beat*) You want that, right? And to get married? Someday? Right?

STEVE: You know I do. I just…business is so bad. I'm glad Dad isn't alive to see what's become of it.

BRYONY: Oh, Steve, he'd be proud of you.

STEVE: No. I don't get it. When we were kids and he was running it, it was glorious. It's like, there were just piles of dead animals everywhere. *(He pauses emotionally.)* It was such a wonderful time.

BRYONY: It will be like that again! I know it.

STEVE: *(Smiling gratefully)* You really believe that?

BRYONY: I do.

STEVE: I don't know what I'd do without you. I love you.

BRYONY: I love you too.

(BRYONY *and* STEVE *kiss. Focus shifts back to the house.* ERICA *sits on the couch, and* MARTY *enters.)*

MARTY: Oh! Good, you're still here!

ERICA: I'm actually going to be staying here. Bryony said I could sleep on the couch. *(She looks at it.)* Is this the same couch that was here when your dad lived here? When we were in high school?

MARTY: The very same.

ERICA: So...this is the same couch we made out on in high school. I remember that night well! I think I sat right here— *(She sits on the edge of the couch.)* —and you were right here. We sat just like this. And...here we are. *(Beat. She sighs.)* Did you think it would be like this?

MARTY: *(Looking at the couch)* What, musty and sinking? Kind of. It's an old couch.

ERICA: No, not the couch. Us. Life. Didn't you think it would...be...more?

MARTY: Ugh, can we not?

ERICA: Not what?

MARTY: Not have that conversation were we reminisce about high school and talk about how crappy our lives turned out. I don't know about you, but my life is... great.

ERICA: Oh yeah?

MARTY: *(With playful, faux pride)* Oh yeah. I'm thirty
years old, I live in a two-bedroom house with my
brother and his girlfriend, and I'm the partial owner of
a nearly bankrupt pet funeral home in the great city of
Beavercreek, PA. This is the dream!

*(ERICA laughs. MARTY stands on the couch and calls out
dramatically.)*

MARTY: I'm living my dream! *(He turns to her.)* Now
you! Be damn proud of your life!

*(MARTY pulls ERICA to her feet, standing on the couch next
to him.)*

ERICA: *(Also with faux pride)* I'm Erica! I'm thirty years
old! I wasted my youth playing murdered sluts in
student vampire films, and spent all my money buying
a trip to Jamaica for me and my boyfriend, who then
decided to go on the trip…with his wife!

MARTY: Oh, man.

ERICA: Now I'm proud to be back in the great city of
Beavercreek, where there is a dead moose in my room,
and I'm trying to figure out…something. Anything.
(She starts to get sad.)

MARTY: No, no, no! Stay proud! Own your crappy life!

ERICA: *(Calling out to the empty room)* I own my crappy
life! *(She laughs.)* And literally nothing else!

MARTY: That's right! No you don't! Me either!

*(MARTY hops down to sit on the couch, and ERICA joins
him. A moment)*

MARTY: Just so you know, I'm, uh, a lot better kisser
now. I've learned some stuff.

ERICA: Well, I hear you've been to jail.

MARTY: That is *not* where I learned stuff.

(ERICA *smiles, and* MARTY *leans in and kisses her.*)

Scene Three

(The pet funeral home. STEVE *stands behind the counter, alone as usual. A silent moment. He looks around to make sure no one is there. He takes a deep breath in, and begins to sing in a high, falsetto voice.)*

STEVE: Ave Mari—

*(*MARTY *enters, drinking a beer.* STEVE *stops singing and snaps back to his spot behind the counter.)*

MARTY: Were you singing?

STEVE: No. Close the door.

*(*MARTY *closes the door.)*

MARTY: You were! You should sing more. You were a kick-ass boy soprano. I always kind of thought that's what you'd end up being.

STEVE: A boy soprano? Yeah, well, who gets what they want in life. Plus, one of us has to show up to work. On time. Without a beer.

MARTY: I'll have you know I've been brainstorming ways to make us a more profitable business. I've been thinking—you know how we charge by the pound for cremations?

STEVE: Yeah?

MARTY: How about, for snakes and ferrets, we charge by the inch? Think about it.

(Beat)

STEVE: You're an idiot. Hey…Erica knows she can't like, *stay with us* stay with us, right? There's no room.

MARTY: Oh, there's no room for Erica, but there's room for forty eggplant penguins?

(Suddenly the bell over the door rings, and MARIANNE
BURK, *an old, old, old woman enters, followed by* FRITZ, *a
tall, handsome, proper gentleman. She has white hair and
walks slowly.)*

MARIANNE: Excuse me, do you do horses?

(Beat)

STEVE: Pardon me?

MARIANNE: Horses. Do you do horses?

MARTY: *(Jumping into action)* Of course we do horses.
(He whooshes over to her and takes her hand.) I'm Martin
Martin, the owner of this business.

STEVE: Partial owner. And I'm Steve Martin.

MARIANNE: Steve Martin! My God!

STEVE: No, no, not that Steve Martin.

*(*MARTY *leads* MARIANNE *to the chairs on the side of the
stage.)*

MARIANNE: I'm Marianne Burk. This is my cabana boy,
Fritz.

FRITZ: *(Patiently sighing)* Your personal attendant,
madam. I wish you'd stop telling people I'm your
cabana boy.

*(*STEVE *gives* FRITZ *a long look.)*

STEVE: You look…really familiar. Have we met?

FRITZ: I don't believe so, sir.

MARTY: Tell us what we can do for you.

MARIANNE: Well, my horse, Sir Trots-A-Lot, is about
to die, and the vet said I should find somewhere to
take him before he dies, because it's much easier to
transport a live horse than a dead horse.

MARTY: Very true. We have a shed out back just for
that. *(Quietly, to* STEVE*)* That's still there, right?

(STEVE *nods.*)

STEVE: We can make him quite comfortable on what's basically an elevator lift up to the…cremation device. It's almost impossible for two men to move a horse once it's passed, but if we can get him there on his own, he'll be quite comfortable.

MARIANNE: It's very sad to think of him like this. He was a prize-winning racehorse in his day.

STEVE: Really?

MARIANNE: Oh, yes!

(MARIANNE *snaps her fingers, and* FRITZ *crosses to her and hands her some faded newspaper clippings.*)

MARIANNE: See? He raced the Kentucky Downs, the Louisiana Downs, all the downs, really. Until he fell down after the Downs Downs.

(*They give* MARIANNE *an inquisitive look.*)

MARIANNE: A charity race for Downs Syndrome. He landed right on top of me—I broke seventeen bones in my body. (*She grabs her kerchief and cries.*) I love that horse!

MARTY: (*Reading the newspaper clippings*) Whoa. He was a huge deal! Is this true? He won over a million dollars?

MARIANNE: Try five million! And even after he fell and couldn't race anymore, he brought in almost a mil a year in stud fees.

STEVE: (*Genuinely perplexed*) Why are you bringing him here?

(MARTY *slaps* STEVE's *arm.*)

MARIANNE: Well, he's from here! I bought him as a young colt just over the hill there. And I want him to rest in his homeland.

MARTY: Of course you do. And you should.

MARIANNE: This horse is my life, and I saw your commercial and I want everything you've got.

STEVE: What?

MARIANNE: Money is no object. This horse made me a very rich woman, and I love him far more than I loved any of my husbands. I want him celebrated and commemorated the way he deserves.

STEVE: Wow. Well, yes, certainly! *(He goes to the counter and gets a clipboard.)* You want him cremated, obviously?

MARIANNE: I want him cremated, and his ashes buried. When my fifth husband died I sprinkled his ashes in the parking lot of the Olive Garden where we met, and I saw a dog literally come and lick him up. That was fine for him, he liked dogs. But I won't have that for my horse.

STEVE: Um, very well. You do know that that will be very expensive, for an animal of that size?

MARTY: *(Under his breath)* Shuuuut it. *(To* MARIANNE*)* Of course. That's the wise thing to do. Now when you say you want all the services—

MARIANNE: I want a funeral service for him. You do funerals?

*(*MARTY *and* STEVE *nod.)*

MARIANNE: Good. And I want everything else you do.

MARTY: Well, we have quite a large catalogue of options. *(He shows her the catalogue.)* You want the pendant?

MARIANNE: Yes.

STEVE: The commemorative T-shirts and mugs?

MARIANNE: Yes.

MARTY: The garden headstone and silver charms with his nose and hoof print?

(MARIANNE *grabs* MARTY *forcefully.*)

MARIANNE: Yes, yes, yes! All of it!

MARTY: Ow! Your arms are…really strong!

MARIANNE: How do you think I get the specimen for my stud fees?! I want everything!

(STEVE *pulls out a calculator and flips through pages and pages of the catalogue, crunching numbers.*)

STEVE: Okay. With the approximate weight of a horse…obituary…funeral service…headstone… tractor equipment for the burial…everything in the catalogue…

MARIANNE: In every color. Guess what my grandkids are getting for Christmas this year.

STEVE: We're looking at about… (*He pales.*) About twenty-five thousand dollars.

MARIANNE: Fine. Do you take cash?

MARTY: Um, yeah.

MARIANNE: I'll have my vet service drop him off this afternoon. Hopefully he doesn't drop dead before then.

STEVE: Very well. If you could just sign this, signing him over to our care.

MARIANNE: I'm leaving town on Saturday, so we'll need to have the funeral on Friday.

STEVE: That's in…three days. Wow, that's a really small window of time to get all of this done—

MARTY: (*Cutting him off*) But it's no problem and we'll be glad to do it. Of course, we'll have to rush order everything, which will cost more. In fact, I'd say it will almost…double the price.

(STEVE *shoots* MARTY *a horrified look.*)

MARIANNE: That's fine. Thank you, boys. (*She gets up to leave, and pats* MARTY *on the face.*) You don't know what this means to me. (*Beat*) Wait until I tell my friends that Steve Martin is cremating my horse!

(MARIANNE *snaps her fingers, and* FRITZ *follows her as she exits.* STEVE *and* MARTY *stand dumbfounded for a moment, then look at each other with wild disbelief. They start to laugh and hysterically high-five each other, dancing around the room.*)

Scene Four

(*The house.* STEVE *and* MARTY *stand center, excitedly talking to* BRYONY, ERICA, *and* TODD.)

BRYONY: Fifty thousand dollars?!

STEVE: That's right! They dropped the horse off this afternoon, and the funeral's on Friday!

BRYONY: Oh my gosh, can I cater it?

MARTY: Yeah you can! This old broad will pay for anything!

TODD: Even getting it taxidermied?!

(*Beat*)

STEVE: Noooo, I think she just wants it cremated.

TODD: Aw, come on! I want on the gravy train! Just let me show her my work, she'll change her mind!

STEVE: (*Changing the subject*) Erica, you want some work for the next few days? We've got a *lot* to do!

MARTY: Funeral Friday, party on Saturday! Whoooo! I'm gonna get my own place and get out of here! This is gonna turn my whole life around!

STEVE: We can move out of this crappy house!

BRYONY: I can quit the diner and start my business! And we can finally get married!

MARTY: *(Carried away)* Hell yeah! You can get married! We can get married! Everyone's getting married!

ERICA: Wait, what?

TODD: Who am I marrying?

MARTY: Got carried away! But they can get married!

BRYONY: *(Hugging* STEVE*)* Oh, finally!

STEVE: *(Awkwardly)* Yeah…!

MARTY: I would like to propose a toast. *(He runs to the kitchen and looks for something to toast with. There's nothing. He finally finds an open can of V8 and pours it into five paper cups.)*

BRYONY: Hey, I was drinking that!

MARTY: Shh, shh, shh. This is a testament to our lives— *(He distributes the cups and holds his aloft.)* —today we drink V8; Saturday, champagne. I would just like to say…it's been a really crappy few years for everyone in this circle. Especially you, Todd. But we've held on, and we've persevered, and it's paid off because things are about to change for us. *(Beat)* Well, not you, Todd, but the rest of us.

TODD: Why am I even part of this toast?

MARTY: I don't know. You're always at our house. Let's raise a glass to…a dead horse!

(Everyone else holds up their glasses gleefully.)

ALL: To a dead horse!

Scene Five

(The pet funeral home, the next morning. MARTY *stands at the counter doing paperwork.* STEVE *enters from the "Employees Only" door, and crosses to* MARTY, *looking perplexed.)*

STEVE: It's still alive.

MARTY: What?

STEVE: The horse. I just went out to the shed to get started and…it's still alive.

MARTY: That's weird. It was barely standing when it got here last night.

STEVE: Well, it's a problem. We can't get started on anything until it…kicks it.

MARTY: Sure we can. I'm halfway through the obit, and Erica is out getting supplies for the funeral.

STEVE: We can't cremate it until after we make the prints, and we can't…

MARTY: You can make the prints now.

STEVE: Not the nose prints. I can't shove a horse's nose into wet cement while it's still alive.

MARTY: *(Shrugging)* Sounds to me like it would solve two problems.

(STEVE rolls his eyes.)

MARTY: Look, we said we do life-to-death transitions. So, transition it. What do you usually do?

STEVE: I…don't want to tell you.

MARTY: Why? Is it gross? I can handle it. I was in the clink.

STEVE: It's just…Dad told me that when you help something pass from one life to the next, you should think about how you'd want to transition. You'd want to be warm, and calm, and feel safe and comfortable. So…I sit next to it and talk to it and pet it.

MARTY: And…?

STEVE: And…light incense and lay a silk sheet on it and play Enya.

MARTY: There it is.

STEVE: I didn't think I'd have to do all that for this one—I thought it would be gone by now.

MARTY: So…transition it a little faster. *(He makes the motion of slitting his throat.)*

STEVE: You are sick. *(He sighs.)* I'll be back.

(STEVE exits. MARTY turns back to the counter, and ERICA enters through the front door, with her arms full of boxes and supplies.)

ERICA: Okay. I got the guest book, the easel for his picture, and Bryony asked me to drop off some of the dishes and serving bowls. She's dropping the rest off in a minute.

MARTY: You can set them right over here. Look, you don't have to help out with this just because Steve asked you to.

ERICA: No, it fits perfectly with the trajectory of my life. I lose everything, move home, and…help organize a horse funeral.

MARTY: Hey, you're a good actress. It will happen for you.

ERICA: Thanks. You're a lot nicer than my last boyfriend. *(She catches herself.)* I mean—not that you're my—I just meant—um, I really don't think it's a good idea, since I just got back to town and all.

MARTY: Did you just start dating me and break up with me in the same sentence?

(ERICA laughs.)

ERICA: Um…

MARTY: *(Smiling)* Well, let me know if you start dating me again.

(MARTY gives ERICA a wink and heads out the "Employees Only" door. When it opens, soft light and the strains of something like Enya's "Only Time" pour through.)

STEVE: *(Offstage)* Close the door!

(The door closes. ERICA stands a moment, smiling to herself. The main door opens, and BRYONY enters, carrying a large stack of chocolate.)

ERICA: Oh! Let me help you with that!

BRYONY: Thank you! *(She sets the chocolate down on the counter.)* Just trying to transport as much as I can ahead of time. Do you think it's bad luck to use a chocolate fountain at a horse funeral that you're also planning on using at your wedding?

ERICA: Um—

BRYONY: I don't think so. *(Beat)* I'm not just like, one of those women who's dying to get married, you know.

ERICA: What?

BRYONY: I know I talk about it a lot, but I'm not that woman.

ERICA: I know. You wouldn't have waited around so long for one guy if you just wanted to get married.

BRYONY: I have my own business, you know? And I'm good. I'm really good. Just you wait until you see this horse funeral. I'm making scallion stallions.

ERICA: Why are you telling me this?

BRYONY: Sorry. I think I just feel…I just know you've been…in the big city, having your exciting life. Being a star, dating exciting men. And you come back here and

I'm…still here. I feel like I haven't made any progress in my life.

ERICA: Well, if dating a guy who turns out to be married and being murdered in six independent films counts as an exciting life, I win. *(Beat)* I was kind of surprised you guys aren't married yet. What's his deal?

BRYONY: He's…a perfectionist. He doesn't want to get married until everything's perfect.

ERICA: Yeah…I'm gonna have to call bull on that.

BRYONY: I would too, but…I don't know. The other option is…he just doesn't want to marry me.

ERICA: Hey, I saw the way he looked at you the other night. He loves you.

BRYONY: I'm really glad this funeral came along, because I was about to… *(Beat)* Never mind.

ERICA: No, this sounds juicy! You were about to what?

BRYONY: I catered this wedding a few months ago, and the bakery that did the cake liked my stuff, and… wanted to go into business with me.

ERICA: That's amazing!

BRYONY: It is! It was completely amazing, but it's in Pittsburg. Like, I'd have to move there. Which is fine if I'm not getting married.

ERICA: You were thinking of leaving?

BRYONY: Well, if he's not gonna propose, yeah! I'm not gonna wait here forever! *(She laughs.)* Just twenty-two years. I have my pride.

ERICA: Well, yeah, twenty-three is the traditional breaking point.

BRYONY: But then his dad died, so I didn't want to leave him. And now, everything's going to be fine.

ERICA: When did their dad die?

BRYONY: Late last year. Get this—he's alive, Steve goes to pick Marty up from jail, by the time they get back, he's dead. I think he just didn't want to see Marty.

ERICA: Oh, come on. Marty's a good guy.

BRYONY: Way down under a thousand feet of crap, you may be right. I'm off to get more scallions. *(She turns to leave.)* Oh, and don't tell anyone about Pittsburg, would you?

ERICA: Of course not.

(BRYONY exits. ERICA turns back to the counter to arrange things. The front door opens and MARIANNE enters with FRITZ.)

MARIANNE: Hellooooo! *(She walks over to ERICA and kisses her on the cheek.)* Hello, Julianne, dear.

ERICA: Do I know you?

FRITZ: I think she's confused—she gets like that sometimes. She thinks you're her daughter. Mrs Burk, I don't think this is Julianne. I believe this is—

ERICA: Erica.

FRITZ: Erica. Hey, Erica. *(A moment as he checks her out.)*

MARIANNE: Fritz, you are an idiot. Julianne, will you please tell Steve Martin that this is the photo I'd like to use for the T-shirts, mugs, calendars, and such?

ERICA: Um, sure. *(She looks at the photo.)* This is a really nice picture of him!

MARIANNE: It was his profile picture on Studfinder. com. *(Beat)* It's like E-Harmony for horses.

ERICA: Great.

(MARTY enters from the "Employees Only" door. Again, something like Enya can be heard.)

MARTY: Mrs Burk!

MARIANNE: I brought the picture you requested. Is he…has he…

MARTY: Yes. He's passed on.

MARIANNE: Oh, Julianne!

(MARIANNE *throws herself into* ERICA's *arms.* ERICA *looks perplexed as she plays along.*)

MARIANNE: Remember the time he kicked over the space heater in the barn? He burned down over seven hundred acres, and all the other animals in the barn were burned to a crisp. But he managed to save himself. He was such a good horse!

MARTY: There, there. We will give him a fitting tribute, I promise you.

MARIANNE: Thank you. *(She starts to leave, then turns back.)* Oh! I wanted to check—I don't know much about these things—is it customary to tip on these kinds of services?

(Beat)

MARTY: Yes. Twenty-five percent…is…customary.

MARIANNE: Glad I checked—I want to make sure to bring enough cash with me.

MARTY: Now you go rest up, tomorrow you can take in the sights of Beavercreek, and we'll see you at noon on Friday.

(MARIANNE *and* FRITZ *head for the door.* FRITZ *exits first.* MARIANNE *lingers a moment, looking around, confused.*)

MARIANNE: Fritz! We're leaving!

FRITZ: *(With a deep sigh, from outside)* I've already left, madam.

MARIANNE: Oh, alright then. Julianne, lay off the cookies, dear. And help me to the car.

(ERICA *complies, begrudgingly, and she and* MARIANNE *exit. As she does,* STEVE *enters from the "Employees Only" door. Soft instrumental music can be heard.*)

STEVE: Who was that?

MARTY: Old broad. Dropped off his picture.

STEVE: Was she upset that he's still alive?

MARTY: I told her he was dead.

STEVE: You what?!

MARTY: If she knew he was still back there, she'd want to go see him! I couldn't let her see your weirdo horse ceremony.

STEVE: Still, that is…unethical.

MARTY: You're right. Guess I'll tell her not to tip us on Friday after all.

STEVE: She's tipping us?!

MARTY: Twenty. Five. Percent.

STEVE: That is…also unethical. (*He heads back to the "Employees Only" door, and sighs.*) I really hope this horse dies soon. My voice is getting really tired from singing all this Enya.

(MARTY *shoots him a confused look.* STEVE *exits through the door. Only once he is through do we hear the vocal line of something like "Only Time" begin again.*)

Scene Six

(*The next morning. The Pet Funeral Home. After a moment,* STEVE *enters from the "Employees Only" door—the soft light and something like Enya play through the door. He looks terrible—he is wearing the same clothes as the day before, his hair is disheveled, he clearly hasn't slept. He*

stumbles over and sits in one of the comfy chairs. A moment.
MARTY *enters, bright-eyed and energetic.)*

MARTY: Good morning! Guess what today is? The last
day we're poor! Whoo! *(He looks over at* STEVE.*)* Whoa,
you look like shit. Long night cremating, huh?

STEVE: No. It's still alive.

MARTY: What?

STEVE: I think…. I think it's getting better. *(He runs his
hands over his face.)* It ate an apple out of my hand.

MARTY: WHY ARE YOU FEEDING IT?!

STEVE: We have to feed it! It's still alive!

MARTY: Well, of course it is, if you feed it!

STEVE: I think…I think we have to start preparing
ourselves that this might not happen.

MARTY: Oh, no. No, no, no you don't. This is
happening. I don't care how it happens, but it happens.
This is the last day I'm poor! THE LAST DAY I'M
POOR!

STEVE: Look—I think we need to call Marianne—

MARTY: We're not doing that—

STEVE: —and tell her the situation—

MARTY: Are you kidding me?!

STEVE: And see what she wants to do.

MARTY: She already thinks it's dead! If we tell her now,
she's gonna sue us! And *if* she doesn't, she's gonna take
it with her on Saturday! And then goodbye, buying
new houses! Goodbye, marrying Bryony and letting
her start her business! Goodbye, awesome speedboat
painted like a shark that Erica and I ride around the
world on while we make love on piles of money!

STEVE: How much do you think we're getting paid?

MARTY: Enough to change it all, man! All of it. *(Beat)* We've gotta kill that horse.

STEVE: Marty—

MARTY: We've gotta do it. We can poison it, we can shoot it—I can hit it with a shovel!

STEVE: Marty...

MARTY: Or, you know, we can just STOP FEEDING IT!

STEVE: —but there is a clear right and wrong here.

MARTY: Is there? Steve, do you really think that horse is going to live much beyond tomorrow anyway?

STEVE: I admit, it seems unlikely—

MARTY: Why not end its suffering while it can still help us?

STEVE: Look—

MARTY: We are good people.

(STEVE gives MARTY a look.)

MARTY: *You* are a good person. And you've been struggling along, doing the right thing your whole life. Where has it gotten you? Really? Where? I mean—is this the life you wanted?

(Beat)

STEVE: No. I wanted to be a boy soprano. But money can't buy that.

MARTY: Look, dreams die. Horses die. Someday, we will die. But for now, we can try to get the life we should have had all along.

(STEVE thinks a moment.)

MARTY: What is the absolute latest that this horse can die of natural causes and we can still pull off this funeral?

STEVE: *(Sighing)* Tonight. If it's gone by…I don't know, eight, and we work through the night, we could still do it.

MARTY: Okay. Okay. I'll give you until eight tonight. And if it hasn't kicked it by then, we can talk again about a new plan. Until then, we prepare as if everything is on track.

(STEVE sighs deeply.)

STEVE: Okay. *(A moment)* Can we not tell Bryony about this?

MARTY: Dude. Minimize the witnesses. I get it. I was in the clink.

STEVE: Not what I meant.

MARTY: I'm gonna go google how to pois— *(He stops himself.)* Minimize the witnesses. *(He turns to leave.)*

STEVE: *(Exhausted)* Close the door.

(MARTY comes back and closes the door. STEVE sighs deeply and runs his hands over his face. BRYONY enters with an armload of dishes.)

BRYONY: Hey, love! *(She sets the dishes down, kisses him on the cheek, and sits next to him.)* You know the horseshoe of roses they put on the winner of the Kentucky Derby? I'm going to make one out of radish roses for the funeral. I'm pretty excited about it.

(STEVE smiles at BRYONY.)

STEVE: How do you come up with these things?

BRYONY: It's no big deal.

STEVE: It is a big deal. I don't understand your brain. Who looks at an eggplant and sees a penguin? Or a radish and sees a rose? You see like, the best version of everything.

BRYONY: Are you ok?

STEVE: I didn't sleep last night. But that's not the point. You just...make everything around you better. Me included.

(BRYONY *is touched.*)

BRYONY: I just like to make things special. That's why I love my business--I get to take special occasions and make them more special. Which reminds me—I gave my notice at the diner today!

(STEVE *pales.*)

STEVE: You what?

BRYONY: Thursday's my last shift! I can't tell you how good it felt—I just walked right up to Marlene and said, "You can take this pepper and stuff it! I'm out of here!"

STEVE: You didn't.

BRYONY: No, that was my dream speech. I chickened out and just said "I quit," but it still felt really good.

(STEVE *glances out at the shed.*)

STEVE: I don't know if that's a good idea...yet...

BRYONY: Why not?

STEVE: I just...don't want you to—

BRYONY: We're about to come into a lot of money. Why wouldn't I quit the diner?

STEVE: You never know what might happen—

BRYONY: What's going to happen?

STEVE: Nothing! I just don't think we should go making any big life plans yet.

(*Beat*)

BRYONY: Like getting married?

STEVE: Like, anything. Look, it's just—

BRYONY: Here we go. It's just what, this time, Steve?

STEVE: It's not like that! Look, the horse isn't—

BRYONY: I have been waiting for you for *twenty-two years*!

STEVE: Can we cool it with that? We couldn't get married when we were ten. So you've only been waiting...like...fourteen years.

BRYONY: You have always said that it was about the money, but you are about to have *lot* of money, so it clearly isn't that. *(She takes a moment to try to keep herself from crying.)* Why don't you want to marry me?

STEVE: I didn't say that!

BRYONY: Well, this sounds like the beginning of a speech I have heard before. You sit around and tell me all these things about how I make you a better man, and it's just words. It's just *words*, Steve! No action! You never *do* anything!

STEVE: You are being really irrational—

BRYONY: *(Screaming hysterically)* YOU'RE BEING IRRATIONAL! *(Beat)* Now, if you will excuse me, I have to go make a dozen horses out of zucchinis. *(She turns to leave, thinks a moment, then turns back.)* You know what? I'm moving to Pittsburg. I'm good at what I do, and I'm moving to Pittsburg. You can take that pepper and STUFF IT!

(BRYONY storms out of the funeral home and into the house. STEVE sits dumfounded a moment. Lights down on the funeral home. In the house, BRYONY paces furiously back and forth. ERICA enters from the outside door, carrying some flowers. BRYONY looks at her a moment, seeing she obviously had a romantic afternoon, and lets out a frustrated grunt.)

ERICA: Jeez! What's wrong with you?

BRYONY: Oh nothing! Just realizing I've wasted my entire life.

ERICA: What's going on?

BRYONY: He's not gonna propose! He all but told me this morning. He has the money, and he's not gonna do it.

ERICA: Are you sure?

BRYONY: Well does, "Uh, um, well", sound like a man who's ready for a lifetime commitment to you? *(A sad beat)* All this time I thought it was the money. He just doesn't want to marry me.

(BRYONY *buries her face in her hands, and* ERICA *comes over and gives her a hug.)*

BRYONY: I told him I'm moving to Pittsburg.

ERICA: Are you?

BRYONY: Well…I guess, yeah! I mean, I mostly said it to hurt him, but I quit the diner and I'm in a dead-end relationship, and… *(The realization sinks in.)* …oh God, I quit the diner and I'm in a dead-end relationship. The room is spinning.

ERICA: Whoa, whoa, whoa. It's gonna be ok. Sit down. You're doing the right thing. Men are the worst.

BRYONY: Shut up. Your arms are full of flowers.

ERICA: Yikes. Sorry. Look, take it from someone who knows. You're gonna be ok.

BRYONY: What are you basing this on? Your house is full of dead animals and you're dating Marty. Are *you* okay? Is *this* my future?

ERICA: Believe me, I hear where you're coming from. But look…Marty's sweet. He's really sweet. I think this could be something for real. He just went to get me a chicken parmesan sandwich. *(As if it's a really big deal.)* *Chicken parmesan.*

BRYONY: *(Wiping her nose)* That's a good sandwich.

ERICA: It's a *really* good sandwich. You want half?

BRYONY: No. I have to go to the market and get more zucchinis for the funeral.

ERICA: You're still going to cater the funeral?

BRYONY: Of course. I can't start my new job in Pittsburg by bailing on a job here.

ERICA: Good point. Here, I'll go to the store with you.

(ERICA grabs her jacket. As BRYONY and ERICA start to leave, MARTY enters with a paper bag.)

MARTY: Hey, there's my best girl! *(He kisses her passionately.)* And here, madam, is your very, very special sandwich.

ERICA: Chicken parmesan, oui, oui!

BRYONY: I'm gonna puke.

ERICA: I'm gonna run to the store with Bryony—just leave it on the counter and I'll eat it when I get back, okay?

MARTY: Your wish is my command!

(MARTY kisses her again, and ERICA and BRYONY exit. MARTY sets the sandwich on the counter. STEVE enters.)

STEVE: Has Bryony cooled off? I need to talk to her.

MARTY: She just left. Why?

STEVE: What?! Where did she go? Pittsburg?!

MARTY: The store. What is wrong with you?

STEVE: *(Really losing it)* This is all your fault! She comes in there, wanting some fancy engagement ring, but I can't promise her one because *the horse won't die,* but *you* already told everyone it was dead, and I can't tell her or she'll get pissed that we lied, but then she thought I didn't want to propose and she got pissed anyway and told me she's moving to Pittsburg!

MARTY: Aww, buddy. Here. I got you this sandwich.

(Beat. STEVE *quietly sits in a chair.)*

STEVE: What am I gonna do?

MARTY: Steve. It's me, Marty! I have a solution to all of these problems.

STEVE: We tell the truth?

MARTY: Of course not. *(He pulls a pamphlet out of his back pocket.)* Have you ever heard of carbon cremations?

STEVE: *(Exhausted)* No.

MARTY: *(Showing him the pamphlet)* It's a process by which super smart science guys extract the carbon from cremated remains, turn them up to a billion degrees, press it together really tight and— *(He pulls a diamond ring out of his pocket.)* —it makes a diamond!

(Beat)

STEVE: What?

MARTY: Todd told me about it this afternoon. Apparently it's his Plan B if the taxidermy doesn't work out. Look, diamonds are made of carbon. Living things are made of carbon. So you can make a living thing into a diamond!

STEVE: How does this help us?

MARTY: Let's say that horse out there doesn't kick it by eight PM. We pretend that it did and hold this funeral tomorrow, and collect our money.

STEVE: That was your plan before!

MARTY: No! In that plan we kill the horse! In this plan, you let that horse live. Hell, feed it apples for another week if it wants! Then, when it dies of its own natural causes, we cash in *again* by turning this horse into like, a thousand diamonds! Who knows how many diamonds you could get out of a horse?!

STEVE: *(Looking at the brochure)* Marty, this costs like a thousand dollars to make a diamond. Who's going to pay more than that for diamonds made of a horse...he asked, as if that were the major hole in this idea.

MARTY: We're not gonna sell them to Zales or somewhere that's gonna verify them. We're gonna sell them on the black market!

STEVE: Of course.

MARTY: We'll take that sixty-five thousand dollars and turn it into a million, at least! They look like real diamonds, right?

(MARTY shows STEVE the diamond.)

STEVE: Where did you get this?

MARTY: Todd—I guess he ordered it online for research. This ring used to be... *(He reads a paper that came with it.)* ...Mrs Sippowitz.

(STEVE tosses it in the air, totally grossed out.)

STEVE: Bleh!

MARTY: Whoa! Careful! He's just letting me borrow it so I can show you! So what do you say?

STEVE: Marty. Every time I think you can't get any more corrupt, you...astound me.

MARTY: *(Touched)* Thank you!

STEVE: No. No to all of this. I can't believe I sat here and listened for this long.

MARTY: Hey, don't decide yet! Just think about it. *(Handing him the ring)* Hold onto it. Look at it. Think about it. And come eight o'clock, if that horse hasn't died, you just ask yourself—would you rather let it

live and turn it into thousands of beautiful diamonds,
or pump its stomach full of gasoline? Those are your
options.

STEVE: Why are those my options?!

*(The sound of a car pulling up outside. STEVE looks out the
window.)*

STEVE: It's Bryony. Get this diamond out of here—if she
sees me holding a diamond ring and it's not for her, it's
gonna be *my* funeral tomorrow.

MARTY: No! Keep it! Think about it!

(MARTY runs out the back door.)

STEVE: I DON'T WANT YOUR DEAD LADY
DIAMOND!

*(BRYONY and ERICA's voices can be heard approaching the
house. STEVE tries to put the diamond in his pocket, realizes
he doesn't have any pockets. He runs in a panicked circle,
trying to figure out where to hide it. ERICA enters, and in a
panic he shoves it into the chicken parmesan sandwich and
strikes a casual pose.)*

ERICA: Hey, Steve!

STEVE: *(His voice all squeaky)* Hey!

ERICA: *(Putting down her groceries)* Look—you really
need to talk to Bryony. But if I were you, I wouldn't do
it right now. The market was out of zucchinis and she
had to go with yellow squash and she is pretty upset.
I'd give her some space if I were you.

STEVE: Good idea. *(He grabs the sandwich and starts to
leave.)*

ERICA: Ha! Nice try. No stealing my sandwich!

(STEVE freezes.)

STEVE: It's my sandwich.

ERICA: No, it's mine. Marty got it for me and left it right there. It's chicken parmesan.

STEVE: *(Rolling his eyes)* Of course he did.

(BRYONY approaches the door, and right before she enters she drops her grocery bag and dozens of yellow squash fall all over the ground.)

BRYONY: *(Bending down to get them, not seeing them)* Ugh!

(STEVE, eager not to see BRYONY, starts to run, but ERICA grabs the sandwich. STEVE silently flips out, but BRYONY stands up and is about to see him, so he runs through the pet funeral home door.)

BRYONY: These cheap bags! Now all these squash are bruised! Look at these! *(She shakes them over her head dramatically.)* I CAN'T MAKE HORSES OUT OF THESE!

ERICA: Honey, you need to calm down. Look, I will pick up all of these squash. You just go lie down, ok?

BRYONY: *(Sighing deeply)* Okay. Okay, I will. Thank you so much, Erica. This is just the worst day.

(BRYONY drops the squash on the floor again and goes to the bedroom. ERICA bends down and collects all of the squash. She takes the bag to the kitchen and sets it on the counter. She sits on a stool and removes the sandwich from its remaining bag/wrapping. She takes a bite. Chews and swallows as normal. She takes another bite and bites down hard on something.)

ERICA: Ow! What the… *(She reaches in her mouth and pulls out the ring. She looks at it a long moment. She goes to the sink and rinses it off.)* Oh my God. Oh my God! Marty!

(ERICA looks at it closely, and tries it on. An emotional moment. She dances around the room, holding the ring up to the light and prancing joyfully. She hears footsteps

*approaching the door and quickly takes off the ring and
shoves it back in the sandwich, then sits nonchalantly.* TODD
enters carrying a taxidermied rabbit. ERICA *is relieved.)*

ERICA: Oh, Todd! I thought you were Marty!

TODD: Nope! Just me! I finished this this morning and
wanted to show the boys! Look!

(TODD *turns it around and* ERICA *gasps. It, of course, is
beyond grotesque.)*

ERICA: Sweet Lord. What happened to it?

TODD: I found it on the side of the road—someone ran
it over. So some parts of it were pretty flat, and some
parts weren't exactly recognizable, but I filled in what
was missing with pieces of that cat I started last week!
See?

ERICA: *(Gagging)* I see.

TODD: But don't you worry. I've got the mess all but
contained to my room and the bathroom now—you
should be able to move back in by next week! You'll
just have to only shower in the front part of
the shower.

(ERICA *smiles mischievously.)*

ERICA: I might not need to.

TODD: No, you will, the back part is full of antlers.

ERICA: *(Whispering)* Todd, can I tell you a secret? I think
Marty's gonna propose.

TODD: Whaaaaaat?

ERICA: He bought me this sandwich, and I just found a
diamond ring in it!

(ERICA *and* TODD *giddily jump around the kitchen in a
circle, both holding hands with the rabbit, squealing.)*

TODD: What a coinkidink…I just *gave* him a diamond ring! Waaaaiiiit—haven't you only been together like… two days?

ERICA: Yeah, but…it's Marty.

TODD: *(Dubious)* And he's proposing by…shoving a ring in a sandwich?

ERICA: Todd. It's *Marty.* And it's a chicken parmesan.

TODD: What are you gonna say?

ERICA: You know…I'm gonna say yes. He's funny, and he makes me feel good about myself, which is a nice change. And after tomorrow he's going to be able to take care of me.

TODD: So, let me see the ring!

ERICA: I put it back in the sandwich—I don't want him to know I already found it!

TODD: Just take it out and let me see it.

ERICA: No, just wait! It's all covered in marinara sauce! I want you to see it nice! *(She heads for the door.)* I can't get engaged wearing this. I'm gonna go buy a new dress. My proposal dress! Eeeee! *(She quickly turns back.)* Oh, and Todd, if you see Bryony, don't mention anything about this, okay? She's having a terrible day, and she and Steve basically broke up this morning, and I think news like this might push her over the edge into some kind of psychotic break.

TODD: *(Stunned)* Really? She and Steve broke up?

ERICA: *(Not hearing or caring)* Stop trying to look in that sandwich! Byeeeee!

(ERICA leaves. TODD sits a moment, then sneakily tries to open the sandwich again. He pokes around in it a little, unable to find the ring. BRYONY enters from the bedroom, wearing a bathrobe and looking terrible.)

BRYONY: Oh, Todd. Hi. Can you get that…thing…off of my counter, please?

TODD: Oh, of course. *(He takes the sandwich off the table.)*

BRYONY: The squirrel, Todd. I meant the squirrel.

TODD: It's a rabbit. With cat features. A cabbit, if you will! Or a…rat.

(BRYONY sits down at the kitchen table and sadly starts to peel the yellow squash. TODD tries to keep sneakily looking in the sandwich as they talk.)

TODD: Listen, Bryony, I heard about you and Steve, and I just wanted to say…I'm real sorry.

(BRYONY's face crumples as she continues to peel the squash.)

BRYONY: Thanks.

TODD: You're a first class lady, and he's a fool if he doesn't want to marry you.

BRYONY: *Thank you! I am* a first class lady! I'm kind, and I can make an animal out of any vegetable. And I just keep thinking, is it something I did? Is it something I didn't do? And you know what? I DON'T THINK I'M THE PROBLEM!

(BRYONY slams the squash down on the table, startling TODD so he drops the sandwich. As she continues to rant, he drops to the floor, trying to clean it up unseen.)

BRYONY: And life is short. And my best years are behind me now, and I spent them with someone who I thought loved me, but must not have loved me after all.

(TODD gets the sandwich cleaned up and leans up to put it back on the counter. He spots the ring on the floor and crawls over to get it.)

BRYONY: And I just want to be with a man, with some balls, who just goes for what he wants, you know?!

(BRYONY turns around just in time to see TODD, kneeling next to her, holding the ring.)

BRYONY: Oh my God.

TODD: What? *(He doesn't get it. Then he looks around, sees his position and the ring, and it clicks. His eyes widen.)* Oh.

BRYONY: Todd…are you proposing to me?

(Beat)

TODD: Okay.

BRYONY: *(Wiping her tears)* You know what? What the hell. Yes. YES!

(TODD looks a little bewildered, but happy.)

TODD: Really?

BRYONY: Sure. What's all over this ring?

TODD: Marinara sauce.

BRYONY: I don't even care. *(She licks it off and puts it on and kisses him forcefully.)* Wanna move to Pittsburg?

TODD: *(Shrugging)* Sure. There's dead animals there too.

(TODD embraces BRYONY joyfully, and STEVE enters.)

BRYONY: Oh, Steve! Hello, Steve. I'd like you to know that *Todd* and I here are getting married.

STEVE: What?

BRYONY: You see, Todd's a man of action, and as soon as he heard we broke up he went out and got me a ring and proposed. Like a *man*!

(BRYONY holds out her hand and STEVE sees the ring. A moment of recognition, then horror.)

STEVE: That's a…nice ring, Todd. Where did you get it?

TODD: It's... (*He looks at the sandwich.*) ...Italian.

BRYONY: You don't even care?! He proposes to the love of your life and you have nothing to say? Punch him, Steve!

TODD: Whoa, what?

STEVE: I'm not gonna punch him! Todd, what is wrong with you?!

TODD: It's my ring! I love her! We both make animals and we're moving to Pittsfield!

BRYONY: Pittsburg.

TODD: I'm too excited! It's all so sudden!

(*ERICA enters and BRYONY holds out her ring.*)

BRYONY: Erica! We're going to be sisters!

ERICA: Why are you wearing my ring?

BRYONY: What?

ERICA: That's...my ring. Todd, what's going on?

TODD: (*Weakly celebratory*) Bryony and I are getting married!

ERICA: What?!

(*MARTY enters.*)

ERICA: Marty! Marty tell them that's the ring you're proposing to me with!

MARTY: Whoahhhhh, what?!

TODD: (*Panicking*) I've gotta go! (*He picks up his rabbit and runs out the door.*)

ERICA: (*Gleefully to MARTY*) You don't have to play dumb! I found it in the sandwich and I say *yes*!

(*ERICA leaps into his arms, and MARTY shoots STEVE a horrified look.*)

BRYONY: *(Confused)* This is my ring and Todd and I are getting married!

ERICA: No, it's mine! Please give me my ring. Tell her, Marty.

MARTY: Steve, what did you do?

BRYONY: Nothing! He never does anything!

ERICA: Give it to me!

(Everyone starts to shout over each other, yelling angrily. TODD meekly sneaks in the front door.)

TODD: *(Quietly)* Guys? *(No one hears him.)* Guys? *(No one hears him.)* GUYS!

(Everyone stops talking and turns to TODD.)

TODD: The horse is gone.

STEVE: What?!

TODD: I just walked by the shed and…it's gone. There's hoof prints leading right outside.

MARTY: That's not possible! How would it have gotten out?!

STEVE: *(Steadily, evenly to MARTY)* Did you close the door?

(Beat)

(Blackout)

END OF ACT ONE

ACT TWO

Scene One

(In the darkness, sets of flashlights appear. All characters wander around a dark stage, searching for the horse. We hear voices in the dark.)

BRYONY: Sir Trots-a-Lot? Where are you?

STEVE: Please come here. *Please!* I'll give you an apple! I'LL GIVE YOU ANYTHING YOU WANT!

TODD: Here, horsey horsey horsey!

MARTY: WHERE THE EFF IS THIS HORSE?!

ERICA: Can we go home? I'm tiiiiired.

(Lights up on stage left, where BRYONY *and* STEVE *search)*

BRYONY: I can't believe you didn't bother to tell me the horse was alive. Oh wait, yes I can, there's a lot of things you don't bother to do!

STEVE: What are we gonna do? I'm getting sued. I'm going to jail. I'm having a nervous breakdown.

BRYONY: You lost your girlfriend today. Does that factor into your breakdown?

STEVE: Well, apparently she had a backup boyfriend, so I think she's fine. By the way, your ring's a dead lady.

(Lights down on them and up on ERICA *and* MARTY *as they search. An awkward moment of silence.)*

ERICA: I was just kidding, you know, when I said I would marry you. I knew the ring was fake, I was just messing with you.

MARTY: Yeah, well, you're like a phenomenal actress, because that was terrifying.

ERICA: Yeah, I bet I made that seem real.

MARTY: You suuuure did.

ERICA: If this was one of my student vampire films, this would be the part where I get murdered, and you'd feel really bad for being mean to me before I died.

MARTY: That would be great.

(Lights down on them and up on TODD, *who sits alone making shadow puppets with his flashlight.)*

TODD: Hey, look, it's a duck! Quack, quack! Haha!

(Lights down on TODD. *Lights up on* ERICA *and* STEVE, *who now search together.)*

STEVE: And I just don't get what she's so pissed about, and Marty's mad at me, and everyone's mad, and I didn't even do anything!

ERICA: I know! And Bryony's all mad that I tried to take her ring, and Marty's like, "I hope you get murdered in the woods," and everyone's mad at me too!

STEVE: I'm not mad at you.

ERICA: Hey, I'm not mad at you either!

STEVE & ERICA: *(Joyfully)* Hey!

*(*ERICA *and* STEVE *hug and the lights go down on them. Lights up on* BRYONY *and* MARTY.)*

MARTY: And I'm like, "Just kill the horse, Steve!" And will he do it?

MARTY & BRYONY: Nooooooo!

BRYONY: And I'm like, "Just propose to me, Steve!" And will he do it?

MARTY & BRYONY: Nooooooo!

(Lights down on them. Lights up on TODD, still alone with his flashlight.)

TODD: Guys? Guys I'm scared! Guys? Neigh! Neigh!

(All the flashlights approach TODD.)

STEVE: It's over here!

MARTY: I hear him!

(They all come in and shine on TODD, who continues to neigh.)

STEVE: Todd! What is wrong with you?!

BRYONY: This is hopeless. We've been searching for hours.

MARTY: It probably wouldn't have gotten as far if someone hadn't been building its strength up with apples.

STEVE: I'm calling it. It's over. We've gotta just come clean and deal with the consequences.

MARTY: That is the *last* thing we should do. We have like, five or six options before it gets to that point.

STEVE: No, Marty! I'm out! I'm done.

BRYONY: What a surprise. (She turns to MARTY.) I'm in. Whatever it is, I'm in.

TODD: Me too! Because we're a couple.

MARTY: Listen—we can still pull this off. *Almost* everything can be done without the horse's physical remains.

ERICA: What about all the nose prints and stuff?

MARTY: It's a good point. We will need some certain animal parts to complete parts of the service. If only we knew someone with access to a lot of dead animal parts. *(He turns and looks at* TODD.*)*

TODD: Oh, no. No, no, no! My animals are for art, not deception!

MARTY: No one could tell a horse nose print from a moose nose print!

TODD: My moose is not for your use!

BRYONY: *(Hitting him in the back of the head)* Come on, Todd! We're a couple!

TODD: Okey-doke.

STEVE: I can't believe what I'm hearing. Have you all lost your minds?

MARTY: Steve, if you'd done the *first* dishonest thing I asked you to do, we wouldn't be in this mess. Now give us the keys to the building and keep your yap shut.

STEVE: No.

MARTY: Steve, you won't survive the clink. You're weak, you won't break rules, and you're named Steve Martin. You'll be dead by lunch the first day. Just hand over the keys.

*(*STEVE *reluctantly tosses* MARTY *the keys.)*

MARTY: Good man! Erica, go get the shirts. Bryony, go get the food. Todd, go get that moose. Steve, we're digging the grave.

STEVE: You said you'd keep me out of it!

MARTY: Dude, I have my own keys. But thanks to these, you're a willing participant, which is what I will tell the police if this thing goes south.

*(*MARTY *and* STEVE *exit.* TODD *turns to* BRYONY.*)*

TODD: Did I show you my duck? *(He holds up his shadow puppet)* There are so many ways to make animals!

Scene Two

*(Later that night. A blank space on the stage that indicates
the pet cemetery near the pet funeral home.* STEVE *and*
MARTY *dig in silence, sweating and working hard.* MARTY
digs the top part of the grave, and STEVE *digs the bottom
part. They dig in a rhythm—their action indicates that*
MARTY *is accidentally throwing dirt back in* STEVE'S *part of
the grave. They work like this for some time.)*

MARTY: Didn't Dad have a tractor that did this?

STEVE: Apparently you have to start it every few years
or it dies out. We haven't needed it.

MARTY: I say tomorrow night, when we have all our
money, we shove that tractor into the middle of the
building and burn the whole thing to the ground. One
last big cremation, eh?

STEVE: We're not burning anything to the ground.
We're keeping it.

MARTY: Keeping it?! We're about to be able to live our
wildest fantasies! In your wildest fantasy, in which we
get filthy rich, you keep running a failing pet funeral
home?!

STEVE: Sixty-five thousand dollars is not as much as
you think it is. We can't just quit our lives.

MARTY: We can, though! Especially if we find that
horse and join the diamond business! We'll never have
to work again!

STEVE: I don't want that! I want to work!

MARTY: Here?!

STEVE: *(Snapping)* IS NOTHING SACRED TO YOU?
(Beat) This was Dad's business! This is all we have left
of him. And you want to corrupt it and burn it and…
charge by the inch for ferrets! He worked hard for this
business. This wasn't just a job to him—it mattered to

him to be able to do something to help people when
they lost their pets. He cared about dignity and respect,
and…he left it to me and I've just run it into the
ground.

MARTY: Us.

STEVE: What?

MARTY: You said left it to you. He left it to us.

(Beat)

STEVE: Sure.

MARTY: Steve?

(A long moment)

STEVE: He didn't leave it to you. He left it to me. Just
me.

MARTY: WHAT?!

STEVE: You were in jail, Marty!

MARTY: That son of a—for selling rain water!

STEVE: No, no, for doing what you always do—
barreling ahead without thinking at all. Of course he
didn't leave it to you.

MARTY: Then why did you tell me he did?!

STEVE: I felt sorry for you! I was afraid if you didn't
have something steady you'd cook up another scheme
and end up back in jail. And yet, somehow I find
myself digging grave for a fake horse funeral!

MARTY: Hey! I am *full* of good ideas for this place!
At least I'm out hustling, trying to make this place
profitable, instead of in the back, throwing froo-froo
death ceremonies!

STEVE: You stop it—*Dad loved those*! He worked really
hard so that nothing ever had to die alone and sad and
scared. And you know what?

MARTY: What?

STEVE: After spending his whole life doing that, guess how Dad died? Alone. And sad. And probably scared. I wanted to be there for him the way he'd been there for all of those animals. But do you know where I was? *(Beat)* Picking you up from jail. Dad didn't get his hand held. He didn't get the incense, or the silk sheet, or the soothing Enya music. He didn't get it any of it, because of you. Because you ruin everything. *(Beat)* All you ever do is make my life harder. Even with Bryony— things with her and I were fine, then *you* show up and give me some corpse ring, and I may have lost her!

MARTY: You can't blame Bryony on me! You had twenty-two years to marry that girl—

STEVE: Fourteen—

MARTY: And you didn't do it. Because—why?! You're not a do-er, man. You're a sitter, and worrier, and a woe-is-me-er. Sitting around feeling sorry for yourself instead of finding any way to solve your life. You wanted to be a singer! What happened to that?

STEVE: That's not realistic.

MARTY: You didn't even try! You had a dream, and you didn't *do* it. You just fell into Dad's old business. Yeah, maybe I come up with a lot of half-baked ideas, but at least I'm doing something! You are your own problem—and I do *not* make your life harder!

(MARTY angrily turns to dig, throwing dirt in STEVE's part of the grave without noticing.)

STEVE: Are you filling my part back in?!

MARTY: Ok, other than that.

(They dig in angry silence.)

Why haven't you married Bryony? Really?

STEVE: I'm going to.

MARTY: Come on.

(*Beat*)

STEVE: I'm waiting. Until she's too old to get pregnant.

MARTY: You don't want her to get fat. I get it.

STEVE: No, it isn't that!

MARTY: You don't want to be a dad?

STEVE: No, I do. I really do. It's just...I don't want her to die.

(*Beat*)

MARTY: Did you miss sex ed day? Because that's not how that works.

STEVE: That's how it worked when mom had you.

(*Beat*)

MARTY: (*Gently*) Steve, come on. You know that—

STEVE: I know that she was here, then you were here, and she was not. I know that our whole lives you were Mr Popular, Mr Funny, Mr Adventure, screwing everything up from the moment you were born, and no one cared. Meanwhile I'm over here cleaning up all of your messes.

MARTY: Yeah, I feel so bad for you, over there as Dad's favorite while nothing I do is good enough for him! Every time I thought I had a great new idea, and this time Dad would be proud of me, it somehow backfired because, oh, I don't know, the pudding cups were expired, or there weren't enough chickens, or there was a different mailman that day.

STEVE: What ideas were these?

MARTY: And then I think, "Wow, well, Dad must have been proud of me on some level, after all, to leave part of his business to me." But he didn't. Because he wasn't. (*Beat*) You think my life is some great time?

Steve. Look at where I am right now. Look at what I'm doing. My life…sucks.

STEVE: I'm in here too. I don't feel bad for you.

MARTY: You know what? You hate me so much? I make your life so hard? Fine. I thought I had some legal obligation here, but I don't. After tomorrow, I'm taking my money and I'm leaving. And you will never, ever see me again.

STEVE: Good!

MARTY: And Bryony's leaving, and Todd and Erica are leaving, so you can just live here all alone with no one to push you to live your life.

STEVE: Sounds good to me.

(MARTY *and* STEVE *angrily dig.* MARTY *again throws dirt in* STEVE's *part of the grave.*)

STEVE: I will kill you.

Scene Three

(*The next day, at the Pet Funeral Home. The room has been set up with a few rows of chairs, facing the center of the room. There is a podium up front, with a large, blown-up picture of Sir Trots-A-Lot perched on an easel. A table to the side is covered in food and horses made of yellow squash.* BRYONY *enters, wearing a T-Shirt with a picture of the horse, and which reads "RIP Sir Trots-A-Lot." She heads over to the food table and rearranges the food, meticulously arranging things.* STEVE *enters, wearing a matching "RIP Sir Trots-A-Lot" shirt. An awkward moment*)

BRYONY: Hello.

STEVE: Hello. (*Beat*) The food looks really amazing, Bryony.

BRYONY: I know. They're gonna love it in Pittsburg.

(Beat)

STEVE: You're not really going, are you?

BRYONY: Yep. Tonight. After I get my money.

STEVE: Look—now you know why I was hesitant to propose. Because the horse wasn't dead. I should have told you. Marty says I…I'm not a do-er. That I just let things happen to me. And I think he may actually be right about something for once. But I'm doing something now. I'm…I'm asking you not to go.

(A long moment)

BRYONY: You're a "do-er" now? Prove it.

(ERICA and MARTY enter, also wearing the shirts.)

ERICA: Okay, I have the rest of it.

(ERICA hands out baseball hats to each of them—each has the matching photo of Sir-Trots-A-Lot.)

MARTY: Ugh. Do we have to wear these?

ERICA: Yes! I drove two hours to pick them up!

(TODD enters, breathless, with a paper bag in his hand. He's wearing a plain white T-Shirt that he clearly tried to draw on with a Sharpie to look like the other shirts. The result is a child-like drawing of a horse, which reads "RIP Sir Shits-A-Lot.")

TODD: *(Panicked, breathless)* You guys! You guys!

STEVE: What are you wearing?!

TODD: Erica said there weren't enough shirts for me, so I made my own! You guys, I s—

MARTY: "Sir Shits-A-Lot"?! What is wrong with you?

TODD: What? *(He reads their shirts.)* Oh, no. I couldn't remember—I knew it was something with diarrhea, and I guessed wrong. The first one I made said Sir Runs-A-Lot, but it's trots! The trots!

BRYONY: It's not the trots! It's trotting! It's just something horses do!

TODD: *(Pointing to his shirt)* So is this. You guys, I—

STEVE: You can't wear that to the funeral.

TODD: What?! This took me all night!

STEVE: *(Looking at how bad it is)* Really?

TODD: No time! You guys, I was on the way over here, and I saw the horse!

ALL: *(Ad lib)* What? Are you sure! Where? Oh no!

TODD: Just over the hill! I was able to catch it—

ALL: *(Ad lib)* Todd! You're amazing! We're saved! You're our hero!

TODD: —but then it got away again when I stopped to pick up some dead birds.

ALL: *(Ad lib)* You idiot! What is wrong with you! You are literally the worst person ever!

MARTY: So it's still just…out there?!

TODD: I guess.

STEVE: We're screwed. If the old lady sees that horse out there, it's over! We're finished! I can't breathe!

(STEVE starts to hyperventilate, and TODD hands him the bag he was holding. STEVE breathes into it, then coughs furiously. When he pulls his face away from the bag feathers billow out around him.)

TODD: Oh, careful, that's full of dead birds. *(He takes out the bag and pulls out an awkward cement shape.)* And the moose nose print!

MARTY: What the hell is this? It doesn't look like anything!

TODD: It looks like a nose print!

ERICA: It looks like a big cement turd, Todd!

TODD: Hey! I shoved a moose's nose in cement for this! And now its nose is rock hard—I can't even taxidermy it!

STEVE: Yeah, it will look so much worse than all your other animals.

TODD: Bryony, are you going to let them talk to me like this?

(BRYONY *looks away, straightening her table again.*)

TODD: I see. You know what? I've had enough of you. Of all of you! I've done nothing but help you all, and all you've done is make fun of my shirt, and get mad at me for losing the horse, and criticize my moose and inhale my birds! Fine. You don't want my help? I'm done. (*He takes back his bag of birds and his moose nose.*) You're all terrible people. (*He turns to leave, and drops his moose nose in the paper bag. It's so heavy that he loses his grip, and the bag lands on his foot, along with six or seven dead birds.*) Ahhhh! Son of a— (*He picks everything up and hobbles out.*)

STEVE: What are we going to do? She's gonna see it! The horse is out there somewhere!

MARTY: We just have to keep her away from the window. If we flip it so the podium is over here, her back will be to the window the whole time. We get her in, do the funeral, get our money, and send her home. Bryony, you got booze over there?

BRYONY: Crown Royal, obviously.

(*Beat, everyone's confused.*)

BRYONY: He was a *crown winner.* Does no one appreciate themes?

MARTY: That's a stretch at best, but it will work. We have to get her hammered. She's leaving tomorrow. Then we're home free! We can do this! Nobody puss

out on me! THIS IS THE LAST DAY I'M POOR! THIS
IS—

(MARIANNE *enters somberly, followed by* FRITZ. *Both wear
the Sir Trots-A-Lot T-Shirt.* MARTY *instantly snaps into his
"swindler mode."*)

MARTY: —a very somber occasion. Marianne—
welcome. Fritz, welcome. Right this way. Please, have a
drink.

(MARTY *hands* MARIANNE *and* FRITZ *glasses.*)

MARIANNE: I don't drink when I'm sad.

MARTY: If I may say so, being sad is the *best* time to
drink.

FRITZ: *(Quietly)* I'll take them. *(He takes both drinks and
downs them.)*

MARIANNE: *(Turning to* ERICA*)* And you shouldn't
drink either, Julianne! You know how you get! No one
needs to see your panties today!

FRITZ: Madam, we've been through this. That isn't
Julianne.

MARIANNE: *(Looking at her closely)* Oh, you're right.
Sorry for the mix-up. My daughter Julianne was
murdered in the woods.

FRITZ: Nope, she wasn't.

MARIANNE: Perhaps I need some air before we start.

(MARIANNE *starts to head for the door, and everyone looks
panicked.* ERICA *jumps into action, racing to* MARIANNE'*s
side.*)

ERICA: *(Altering her voice)* Mama, it's me, Julianne.
Come sit next to me.

STEVE: *(Frantically whispering)* What are you doing?!

ERICA: *(Hissing back)* A daughter who was murdered in the woods? I'VE BEEN TRAINING FOR THIS ROLE MY WHOLE LIFE!

FRITZ: Um—

MARTY: *(Handing FRITZ another drink)* It's all part of the service, comforting the grieving. No harm done. Don't worry about it; have a drink.

(FRITZ downs another drink, and ERICA leads MARIANNE to the front of the room to look at the large picture of the horse.)

MARIANNE: He was so beautiful. Remember when he kicked you and broke your collar bone, Julianne?

ERICA: Um, yes.

MARIANNE: And everyone said he had done it on purpose because he was a mean, spiteful horse. And he did. But I think you deserved it, Julianne. You really did.

ERICA: *(Bewildered)* Yes, mama.

MARIANNE: Can we get started, please?

MARTY: Of course. Everyone, please take your seats.

(All head to their seats, FRITZ stumbling a bit drunkenly to his. ERICA sits next to MARIANNE.)

MARTY: We are gathered here today in memory of Sir Trots-A-Lot, a truly magnificent horse.

(MARTY nods to STEVE to start the music. STEVE pushes play on an old CD player, which begins playing an obnoxious mariachi song. STEVE looks panicked and pushes the "next" button, and a rock song comes on. STEVE panics again and goes to the next track, which is somber organ music. He breathes a sigh of relief. MARTY rolls his eyes.)

MARTY: Sir Trots-A-Lot lived a full life. He was born right here in Beavercreek, but went on to conquer the world. He will be remembered as a first-class racehorse, the father to…many, and a dear friend to his beautiful owner, Ms Marianne Burk.

(MARIANNE *nods somberly.*)

MARIANNE: If I may, I'd like to say a few words.

(MARIANNE *stands up to go to the podium, and a wave of panic goes through the room—at the podium, she'll be facing the window.* MARTY *shoves her back down.*)

MARTY: Of course. But first…your daughter… Julianne…would like to say a few words.

(ERICA'*s eyes widen, and* MARTY *yanks* ERICA *to the podium. She stands there a moment, terrified.*)

ERICA: *(In her altered voice)* What can one say about Sir Trots-A-Lot. He was…a horse. A white horse. He had two ears, and two eyes. He had four hoofs, and…a tail….and apparently broke my collar bone once. But I deserved it. Because he was a good…fast…horse.

(*As* ERICA *speaks,* FRITZ *has wandered over to the food table next to* BRYONY *and* STEVE, *and is pouring himself another drink.*)

FRITZ: *(Drunkenly reading the bottle)* Crown Royal. Oh! Because he won so many crowns!

BRYONY: Yes! THANK YOU!

(FRITZ *downs another one.*)

FRITZ: Is that a scallion stallion?

BRYONY: YES!

FRITZ: You should drizzle it in Italian dressing. Make it an Italian Scallion Stallion.

BRYONY: Maybe I'll add it to my menu in Pittsburg! I love that!

FRITZ: I love you. I'm pretty drunk.

BRYONY: Ya think?

FRITZ: These are amazing. You're amazing.

(FRITZ leans in towards BRYONY, and STEVE steps between them.)

STEVE: Okay, that's enough of that.

(BRYONY shoots STEVE an icy look.)

BRYONY: You don't like it? What are you gonna *do* about it?

(They shift their focus back to ERICA.)

ERICA: *(Breathy)* So in conclusion, Sir Trots-A-Lot was a tall horse, with teeth. And he will be missed.

(ERICA rushes to her seat.)

MARIANNE: Julianne, that was terrible, just like everything you've ever done. And now I'd like to say a few words— *(She starts to stand.)*

MARTY: But first, Fritz would like to say a few words! Fritz! Get up here!

(FRITZ looks up from his eating, and, taking a squash horse with him, stumbles to the front. MARIANNE sits down again.)

FRITZ: *(Gnawing on a squash and leaning on the podium)* This horse was a pain in my ass.

MARIANNE: Fritz!

FRITZ: He was. I got up at five to feed this thing, and it bit me *every morning*. You think he was named Sir Trots-A-Lot because he was a runner? No, it's because he had worse diarrhea than any animal that ever lived.

MARIANNE: That's true.

FRITZ: And who cleaned it up? *Me!* This was a mean horse with an ice-cold heart. He would look in my eyes, and I could feel him stealing little pieces of my soul. He would just suck it up through his devil nostrils. And even now, I can't believe he's gone. I look out that window, and I swear, I still see him.

(BRYONY *looks out the window and gasps audibly—the horse is clearly out there.*)

FRITZ: That's right! Run! Just keep prancing, you bastard!

MARIANNE: For Pete's sake, Fritz, sit down. You're embarrassing yourself.

(*Ushering* FRITZ *away from the podium:*)

MARTY: Fritz is overcome with grief delirium. Happens to us all. Go have a lie down, Fritz!

(FRITZ *stumbles back to the food table and puts his arm around* BRYONY. STEVE *seethes.*)

MARIANNE: Now, if I may say a few words—

MARTY: No! You can't! Not right now!

MARIANNE: Why on earth not?

MARTY: Because…because…

(STEVE *stands triumphantly in the back.*)

STEVE: Because I haven't sung my song!

(*A moment, all eyes on* STEVE, *shocked.*)

MARIANNE: Oh, how wonderful! Steve Martin is going to sing at my horse funeral!

(STEVE *takes a deep breath—it's as if something has come over him, and he has embraced his destiny. He slowly walks to the front of the room, proudly and with purpose.*)

STEVE: I am very proud to sing here today. This is for my mom, and dad. And for you, Bryony.

(MARTY *clears his throat and shoots* STEVE *a look.*)

STEVE: And you…Sir Trots-A-Lot.

(STEVE *snaps his fingers and* MARTY *presses "play" on the boom box. An instrumental version of "Ave Maria" begins.* STEVE *snaps his fingers at* ERICA, *who is confused. He snaps more impatiently and she turns on her flashlight and shines it on him, creating his own spotlight.* STEVE *closes his eyes, and begins to sing in a ridiculously high voice.*)

STEVE:
Ave Maria, gratia plena
Maria, gratia plena
Maria, gratia plena
Ave, ave dominus,
Dominus tecum.
Take it, Marty.

(STEVE *closes his eyes with emotion.* MARTY *looks panicked, wanders to the front, and starts to sing, also in a ridiculously high voice. He clearly doesn't know the words, and is just singing nonsense words.*)

MARTY:
Ave bageera…gracias amigo
Maria, I just met a girl named
Maria, obla dee, obla dah
Macarena, dominos
Dominos scrotum.

(*As he sings,* FRITZ *continues to drink.* FRITZ *looks out the window and points.*)

FRITZ: I'm not horse! That drunk is really out there!

(*A panicked moment.* BRYONY *shoves* FRITZ *towards the door.*)

BRYONY: Well, go get it then!

(*She pushes* FRITZ *out the door and he drunkenly stumbles away. She turns back to watch* STEVE *sing.*)

STEVE: (*Whispering*) Close the door!

(BRYONY *closes the door, then watches* STEVE, *enraptured by his performance.*)

STEVE:
Ave Maria, gratia
plena Maria, gratia
Maria, gratia plena
Ave, ave dominus,
dominus tecum.

MARTY:
Ave papaya, gracias amiga
Maria, I just met a girl named
Maria, gracias amiga
YMCA, dominos
dominos scrotum.

(The song ends. A moment of silence. BRYONY *applauds wildly;* STEVE *bows as if he has given the performance of a lifetime. The rest look around awkwardly.)*

MARIANNE: What the hell was that? *(She starts to stand.)* I am going to speak now.

MARTY: No, you—

MARIANNE: You hush up! This has hardly been the funeral I imagined for my beloved horse, but I am going to speak now and I would thank you to sit down and let me pay my respects.

*(*MARIANNE *heads up to the podium.* MARTY *rushes up and puts one of the baseball hats on her.)*

MARTY: Don't forget your hat.

*(*MARTY *tilts it down so the brim is over* MARIANNE's *eyes.)*

MARTY: This is how all the kids wear them now.

*(*MARIANNE *takes it off and throws it on the ground.)*

MARIANNE: No.

(A moment. Everyone waits nervously.)

MARIANNE: Sir Trots-A-Lot was my best friend. I have not lived a life where many people liked me, or understood me. But my horse did. Many people said that he was a mean-spirited horse. But I knew he was not. Sometimes, at night when I couldn't sleep, I would go out to the barn and just talk to him. He would listen…unlike most people. He didn't judge me, or yell at me, or try to take my money. He just…loved me. In his quiet way. And it's rare to find love in this life. If you can find it, you hold onto it.

(STEVE *and* BRYONY *look at each other.* MARTY *and* ERICA *exchange a look.*)

MARIANNE: I will miss him more than I can possibly say, and— (*She pauses a moment, squinting at the window.*) What the—

(MARTY *nervously starts to stand up.*)

MARTY: Um—

MARIANNE: Oh my God!

(MARIANNE *starts to walk towards the window, and right as she approaches it, a large animal head resembling a horse comes in through the window, inches from her face. She lets out a blood-curdling scream.*)

MARIANNE: AAAAAAHHHHHHHHH!

(*Blackout*)

Scene Four

(*The Pet Funeral Home.* FRITZ *pulls a white sheet over* MARIANNE's *body on a stretcher as* STEVE, MARTY, ERICA, BRYONY, *and* TODD *stand with shocked expressions on their faces.* TODD *holds a grotesque taxidermied head—the one that came through the window—in his arms.*)

TODD: I just wanted to show her my work. I was so mad at you guys, I wanted to tell her the horse was alive and convince her to let me taxidermy it when it died. (*Beat*) Do you think it was so lifelike that she thought it was really her horse?

(*Beat*)

ERICA: I really don't think that's what happened.

MARTY: *(Looking at it)* More like she thought it was her actual horse that had been dead for days come back from hell to haunt her.

STEVE: It doesn't even look like a horse.

TODD: It isn't a horse. It's a number of animals combined, including my moose, to have horse-like features. It was a prototype.

FRITZ: Excuse me. I'll be back.

(FRITZ wheels the stretcher out of the room. Everyone stands in silence a moment.)

BRYONY: It feels so weird to have death in this room.

MARTY: Look, she was old. She got surprised. Same thing would have happened if she walked out of here and a bird spooked her. Or she fell down an elevator shaft. Or she choked on a popcorn kernel. There's a million ways to die, and seeing a fake horse head is one of them.

TODD: I have to do some thinking. My art was meant to preserve life, not take it away. Bryony? Can I talk to you a moment?

(BRYONY cautiously crosses to TODD.)

TODD: I'm very sorry, and please don't become hysterical, but...I am calling off our engagement.

BRYONY: *(Stiffly)* Are you sure?

TODD: I've been thinking about this ever since Marty mentioned all those ways to die.

MARTY: Really? Ever since then?

TODD: Life is short, and I have to listen to my heart. Especially because its beats are often irregular thanks to the taxidermy chemicals in my bathroom. I think, deep down, you love someone else.

BRYONY: You may be right, Todd.

TODD: I saw how you looked at him when he wheeled the old lady out. I give you my blessing. May I please have Mrs Sippowitz back?

(BRYONY *looks confused a moment, then realizes and takes off her ring. She hands it to* TODD.)

TODD: I'll never forget the beautiful life we could have had, making animals together.

(TODD *leans in to kiss* BRYONY, *who tries to tastefully resist. He tries a few more times and then gives up.*)

TODD: I understand. It's too painful. (*He exits, dragging his animal head behind him.*)

MARTY: So I guess we're not getting paid, huh?

STEVE: Well, worse than that. Now I'm responsible for all of these expenses.

MARTY: So, we *lost* money on this.

STEVE: Yeah. Like…all of it. It's gonna sink us.

(*A somber moment*)

STEVE: You know what? I'm glad we're not getting all that money. We all became awful people from the moment that old lady walked in our door. (*He turns to* BRYONY.) But I'm kind of glad, because being up there today, singing, was the most alive I've felt in my whole life. I *did* something. And it makes me want to do other stuff. (*He takes her hand.*) I thought I needed all that money to make a life for us. And I was scared that I'd impregnate you and you'd die.

BRYONY: Wait, what?

STEVE: But you know what? You can get startled by an animal carcass and die. Life is short, and I've been stuck in neutral. I have less to offer you now than I have ever had before, and if you want to move to Pittsburg and do your business without me, I understand. And you should. You're amazing. But Bryony, if you can ever forgive me, I want to go with you. And marry you.

BRYONY: *(Very touched)* Of course I'll marry you. *(She throws her arms around him.)* But please propose for real later. I can't tell my mother you proposed to me at a horse funeral.

MARTY: You know what? I want you to add me as part owner of this place. For real.

STEVE: *(Skeptically)* Why?

MARTY: Because...if you're in crazy debt over this scheme, then I am too. Plus I really want to stick it to Dad. *Now* who's a responsible son?!

(MARTY extends his hand, and STEVE, touched, shakes it.)

BRYONY: You know what? Add me, too. We're family.

(A moment. STEVE is very touched. They all look at ERICA, who puts her hands up.)

ERICA: Hey, I've been here for like two days. We're not family.

(FRITZ re-enters.)

FRITZ: I found the horse running around out there. I caught him and stuck him in that shed out back. He's pretty worked up—I lit some incense and he calmed right down. That's...weird that you have that out there.

STEVE: Fritz, we are so, so sorry about this.

(FRITZ holds out his hand.)

FRITZ: Augustus.

STEVE: I'm sorry?

FRITZ: I'm not Fritz. I'm Augustus.

MARTY: I don't get it.

(FRITZ *turns to* ERICA.)

FRITZ: Are you Julianne?

ERICA: No.

FRITZ: I'm not Fritz. Same thing. *(He turns to leave.)*

STEVE: Whoa, whoa, whoa! What are you talking about?

FRITZ: The real Fritz has been dead for years. I found him in an upstairs bathroom when I came to fix the plumbing. I came downstairs, she called me Fritz, I just kind of went with it.

MARTY: Why?!

FRITZ: *(Shrugging)* I always wanted to be an actor. I even had a challenging duel role when she asked me to scope this place out.

STEVE: What do you mean?

(FRITZ *assumes the posture of* MARCUS.)

FRITZ: *(As* MARCUS*)* Dude, she like, wanted me to check you out and see if you were like, as good as you seemed on your commercial.

MARTY: *I knew it!*

STEVE: *(Overjoyed, to* BRYONY*)* He came back!

FRITZ: *(To* STEVE*)* But you were so kind to me that day—why, if you hadn't given me that free casket, we never would have come here.

(*Everyone glares at* STEVE.)

STEVE: Great.

FRITZ: But now, guess maybe I'll try being an actor for real. Seems glamorous.

ERICA: I did some acting. Believe me, it's not.

FRITZ: Hey, I knew you looked familiar! You were in *Forest of Screams*!

ERICA: You saw that?!

FRITZ: That was only the best on-screen woods death ever! Do it, do it!

(ERICA *pretends she's being strangled.*)

FRITZ: Oh, man. You're amazing! Do you want to like, get a burger or something?

ERICA: *(Looking at* MARTY*)* Oh, I don't know.

FRITZ: I mean, I have to swing by the attorney's office and pick up my inheritance first, but then I can go.

(ERICA *looks at* FRITZ *inquisitively.*)

FRITZ: She left all her money to Fritz.

ERICA: Um, yeah, I can definitely get a burger.

STEVE: Are you kidding me? You get all her money?

FRITZ: *(Shrugging)* Fritz does.

MARTY: Look, Fritz—Marcus—Augustus—buddy. Maybe you can help us out. We just went in a huge hole over this funeral—maybe you can use some of that money and dig us out? So to speak? Solidarity? Everyone trying to swindle an old lady together?

FRITZ: Yeah, except I was good at it. *(He extends his arm.)* Julianne?

ERICA: Fritz!

(ERICA *and* FRITZ *start to exit.*)

MARTY: Are you kidding me?!

ERICA: Hey, Marty. You were right—my acting career did work out! Good luck with everything here! *(She pats him on the back.)* Own your crappy life!

(ERICA *runs out.* MARTY *stands dumbfounded a moment.*)

MARTY: What?! *(He crosses and sits in the chair next to* STEVE *and* BRYONY.) Now what?

(A long moment.)

STEVE: We get what we deserve, I guess.

BRYONY: We'll be ok. We're family, and we have each other.

MARTY: Oh shut up. We're going to the poor house. *(A moment.)* What's that smell?

(They all sniff the air. They definitely smell something.)

STEVE: What is that? Is that the incense?

(They stand and sniff, following their noses around the room. They all end up near the "Employees Only" door. STEVE *opens it and looks out.)*

STEVE: Oh my God! The shed! The shed is on fire!

BRYONY: What?!

STEVE: The incense! The horse must have kicked over the incense! That effing horse! Call the fire department! Oh my God! *(To* BRYONY*)* Bryony, go save things from the house!

*(*BRYONY *runs through the joint door and tears around the house.)*

STEVE: I have to try to put it out!

*(*MARTY *calmly grabs* STEVE'S *arm.)*

MARTY: No, wait.

STEVE: *(Hysterical)* It's gonna burn down! Go, go, go! We have to put it out!

*(*STEVE *starts to run out and* MARTY *pulls him back.)*

MARTY: Steve—what if you do what you do best? Do… nothing?

STEVE: Then it will burn to the ground! The funeral home, the house!

MARTY: What's the insurance money on this place?

STEVE: No, no, no! This was Dad's business! Dad's house!

MARTY: Steve—look, he's gone. After today, we're gonna lose the house and the business either way!

(Beat)

STEVE: So we just…do nothing.

MARTY: Do nothing.

(BRYONY *runs back in.*)

BRYONY: I couldn't find anything I wanted to save!

STEVE: Marty seems to think…that there is a nice insurance policy on this place. And that I should do nothing.

(BRYONY *looks confused, then her eyes widen in realization.*)

BRYONY: Ohhhh…you *should* do nothing!

(BRYONY *takes* STEVE'S *hand. A long moment*)

STEVE: No. I'm not a guy who does nothing anymore. I'm not gonna do nothing.

(MARTY *and* BRYONY *sigh.*)

STEVE: I'm gonna throw one last transition ceremony. For this business. And for Dad. Get my silk sheet!

(BRYONY *and* MARTY *smile, and* BRYONY *gets one from behind the counter.* STEVE *drapes it over his shoulders.*)

STEVE: The incense is…already burning. So all we need is—

(STEVE *pushes play on the CD player, and* Orinoco Flow *by* Enya *plays. He moves to the center of the room with* MARTY *and* BRYONY. *He raises his hands and sings a few lines of the song.*)

STEVE:
Sail away, sail away, sail away—

(STEVE *motions for* MARTY *and* BRYONY *to join him, and they do, reluctantly, rolling their eyes a bit.*)

MARTY, BRYONY & STEVE
Sail away, sail away, sail away—

STEVE: Dad—we thank you for the privilege of running your business. We hope to give it the kind of passing you didn't receive. We honor the legacy you left in this building, and we…apologize for like, completely desecrating that in its last days. Marty?

MARTY: *(Looking around)* Dad…you were right not to leave me this business. I've been part-owner for ten minutes and it's literally burning to the ground. Bryony?

BRYONY: *(Looking around)* Mr Martin…you gave a lot to this earth, including two really unfortunately named sons. But they're my family…and I'm grateful.

(BRYONY *takes* STEVE *and* MARTY'*s hands.*)

STEVE: And now we shall sing— *(He looks towards the "Employees Only" door, which is lit orange.)* Oh, jeez. It's really moving fast. We've gotta go.

(*The three of them turn to go.* BRYONY *takes one of her zucchini horses, and* STEVE *grabs the large photo of Sir Trots-A-Lot. He kisses her, and they turn to exit. He points out the door.*)

STEVE: Hey, look. There goes the horse. Still alive.

(*They exit.* MARTY *takes a moment and looks around, really touched.*)

MARTY: Bye, Dad.

(*He exits.*)

STEVE: *(From offstage)* Close the door!

(*Blackout*)

END OF PLAY

www.ingramcontent.com/pod-product-compliance
Lightning Source LLC
Chambersburg PA
CBHW052205090426
42741CB00010B/2410